LANDFALL 235

GW00383935

May 2018

Editor Emma Neale
Founding Editor Charles Brasch (1909–1973)

Cover: Kathryn Madill, *The House Party*, 2018, monoprint, 320 x 430 mm.

Published with the assistance of Creative New Zealand.

ARTS COUNCIL OF NEW ZEALAND *TOI AOTEAROA*

OTAGO UNIVERSITY PRESS

CONTENTS

LANDFALL REVIEW

EMMA NEALE

Charles Brasch Young Writers' Competition 2018 Judge's Report

There was a slim crop of essays this year: at just 26 entries, the intake was about half the size of the inaugural year's mushrooming. Surprisingly, given the smaller batch of entries, there were still some recurrent topics. One was the nature of mental health; another was how to reconcile individual and broader cultural identity. This latter subject was covered in a number of different ways: from what a sense of national identity might mean to a Pākehā New Zealander, to life here as an immigrant, and to some of the perhaps unexpected internal complications of being bilingual.

Further entries covered everything from NCEA set texts to the traumatic memory of a car accident; from tensions in friendship to what it means to be a member of the #NeverAgain generation, even for someone geographically removed from the United States; and to the nature of language change over time. There were a couple of instances of genre confusion. Some writers submitted fiction and poetry that didn't consciously engage with the aims an essay might have. Although I was prepared to have walls around genre blown down, I think these entries were probably a case of good writers not reading the competition rubric closely enough, rather than iconoclasts blasting through the boundaries of tradition.

Third place goes to 'The Rat without a Shadow' by **Rata Quark**: a powerful, fiercely intelligent memoir charting the writer's turbulent adolescence, where social frictions and immense personal frustration stemmed from a delayed diagnosis of autism spectrum disorder. The essay argues persuasively that the gendered assessment criteria for ASD were a major obstacle in the author arriving at a sense of identity: 'I am a skeuomorph woman.' 'I am … a rat armed with words.'

Janna Tay's 'Bodies in the Land', the best exploration of the layers in cultural identity, gained second place, with its remarkable range of aesthetic virtues: a combination of everything from a vividly sensuous rendering of the differences between Malaysia and Auckland, to the more philosophical explorations of the formation of identity and notions of home for someone raised in three languages (Hokkien, Mandarin and English), and who, as Malaysian Chinese, is often 'othered' by a dominant and frequently dismissive white gaze. 'This is what I have lost: gravity, a provenance. A name with meaning and people who see beyond my race.' Yet Tay skilfully and optimistically also charts internal change; this essay compresses considerable depth and distance into its short form.

The author of the winning essay, 'Disappearing Disease', shares the second place-getter's ability to combine the concrete, grounding specifics of time, place and context with a broader recognition of pressing global concern. **Aimee-Jane Anderson-O'Connor** notices a cluster of dead bees in her shared student flat; from this she lightly explores mythology and entomology, stirring facts and legend together into a piquant golden melt, honey and salt, always keeping the widening knowledge of bee facts held in a fine net of sharp and particular description.

With bright imaginative patches, the writing gently, and often humorously, melds human and animal worlds, yet also allows for the dark undertow of increasing ecological threat: 'I felt like a murderer, a murderer with a melted popsicle and big hoofing feet.' 'Flies rubbed their grubby hands together, teamed up and flew at them, chased them into corners of the room.' 'I keep thinking about the queen bee and I wonder if she ever finds it hard to wake up in the morning. If she ever wants to just turn off the news. I wonder if she wonders whether she should really bring more bees into the world.'

Anderson-O'Connor's compelling ability to foxtrot through several tonal changes, yet also inform the reader, show an artistic maturity and agility that it has been energising to see.

Aimee-Jane Anderson-O'Connor wins $500 and a year's subscription to *Landfall*. Her prizewinning essay follows.

Disappearing Disease

There is a bee graveyard behind our kitchen curtain. Fifteen winged bodies curled in the foetal position, fuzzy and grey and sunk on the white sill. We figure our flat is in the way of some ancient migratory course; we figure that while we go to work they trail in through the latched window and buzz a slow circuit behind the netting. Too drunk on the student smells of Ajax and Lynx to realise they're drowning.

They say that bees have been around since the Garden of Eden, that they are the servants of God. Their honey is ambrosia, the nectar of immortality, mead, a natural antiseptic, $11.99 a jar at Pak'nSave. Some say that a bee circling a sleeping child signals a long and happy life. Others reckon that bees are the messengers of the dead. In the hive, select worker bees spend their lives as undertakers, removing the striped corpses of their cellmates. When you go to a funeral, you must tell the hive of your loss. You should repeat the news three times. You should make them a cup of tea, and tell them gently. You should bring them back one of those little cucumber and tuna sandwiches.

This weekend twenty of them sailed into our kitchen while my flatmate cooked stir-fry. They kept trying to dive-bomb the peanut sauce and she kept yelling about how she wanted to kill them all. The slaps of the spatula hit the walls. We told her not to worry, that they were sure to add protein to her lunch, and after all, stings help with arthritis later. Noodles stuck and burnt to the bottom of the pan, the whole room silver smoke. I imagined bees hitting the element and catching fire. Flying, still flaming, burrowing under the carpet and smoking, turning our house to ashes. I grabbed a sticky McDonald's cup from the table and trapped a worker against the wall. Slid a Pizza Hut flyer under the lip and shuffled her vertical until I could flip the cup like an amateur magician. I shimmied the back door open with my elbow and held her above the cherry tomatoes.

Flourished the flyer, saw how I saved us with a flick of the wrist.

When I was about five, I stepped on my first ever bee. Dad says I lumped down onto the grass and quietly cried. He flicked the sting from my foot and told me not to worry, that the bee would also suffer, that she'd left half her tummy behind with the sting, and would die soon and so could not come back and do it again. I thought about her gasping through the grass, cold and alone. I felt like a murderer, a murderer with a melted lemonade popsicle and big hoofing feet. When a bee feels threatened, it releases alarm pheromones to warn its fellows and implore them to defend the hive. In some species this pheromone smells like banana. This is why beekeepers billow smoke into hives. I thought it was just like incense, and lulled them to sleep, but really it just muffles their cries for help.

The bees plagued our kitchen all afternoon. They threw themselves at the glass, battled through our netting, crawled under the gap in the door. They seemed lost and frantic. Flies rubbed their grubby hands together, teamed up and flew at them, chased them into the corners of the room. The bees fought them off, then collapsed on the floorboards, exhausted. They looked less menacing there on the ground. Like somehow they had less sting. We picked them up with a teaspoon. Placed them under the grapevine, on a saucer filled with sugar water.

We watched this documentary about bees to see how we could help them. We learnt that there used to be a thing called Disappearing Disease that happened every now and again, where a hunk of bees would just disappear to die. There would be no signs of struggle, no bodies, just the queen and a handful of her attendants slowly starving. In 2006 one-third of all the bees in the United States disappeared, and thousands of colonies around the world started to keel over. People wondered if it was because of cellphone signals or a bee version of Aids. Scientists thought it might be because of malnutrition, pesticide, a mite or parasite. They performed autopsies and scooped up dying bees in measuring cups. Found white sacs of fungi like pus in their guts. They put struggling hives under quarantine, even though they didn't really have to. The bees would hardly move, and even their most sworn enemies left them alone. The scientists discovered this thing called Israeli Acute Paralysis Virus, but they say that this still doesn't account for all of it. They say it's probably a lot of different things hitting the fan. Bee numbers across the world continue to decrease.

Dusk settled in and still they kept coming. I called my grandfather, who used to keep bees with his friend in Newstead. He said we should only be worried if they start to swarm. *That, he said, would mean you might have the queen somewhere in the house.* I stood there at the sink and thought about where she might be. Behind the oven. In the Tupperware cupboard, the cutlery drawer. Grandad said *if this is the case, then perhaps you ought to move out.* We laughed down the line. They would arrive like a great humming cloud. They could build their combs through our house. Defend us from StudyLink. Fill our walls with clover honey.

Usually, bees get their necessary water intake from nectar. However, very occasionally, in extreme weather, bees will deviate from their usual paths in search of water. This was the hottest summer we've had in New Zealand. We knew this was coming. We've heard what Einstein said. Bees pollinate about a third of the world's food sources. No bees – no honey, no fruit, no veges, no nuts, no cotton. On average, the queen bee lays 2 million eggs in her lifetime.

I couldn't find fresh spinach anywhere in Hamilton last Wednesday. The last male northern white rhino died this week. In Auckland, one head of broccoli currently costs $10. I keep thinking about the queen bee and I wonder if she ever finds it hard to wake up in the morning. If she ever wants to just turn off the news. I wonder if she wonders whether she should really bring more bees into the world.

I end the call and hear buzzing from the sink. There's this bee with her legs caught in the strainer, and she thrashes against the metal, thunks her wet body in the drain. She stills, then crawls out onto the bottom of the sink, clings to a drift of potato peel. I fetch the cup and reach out to save her, but another bee hums on my cheek and I flinch, tense, accidentally press the cup down and cinch the sink bee at the waist. She crackles like static and my eyes prickle. A dollop of venom, orange like raw pumpkin. She limps and tries to scale the sink wall. She can't do it. I watch her gasp. I think about turning the tap on full.

I don't. I take the flyer and slip it under her, real gentle. Place her on the windowsill to rest. She begins to curl. The outside air ripples on her wings.

SOURCES
'Bee-keeping in New Zealand', Ministry of Agriculture and Fisheries New Zealand, *Bulletin* 267, 1975.
Megan Gattey, 'It was officially New Zealand's hottest summer on record': www.stuff.co.nz/
    environment/101996439/it-was-officially-new-zealands-hottest-summer-on-record
Doug Schultz, 'Silence of the Bees', from *Nature* documentary series, PBS San Diego, 2007.

CALLING ALL ESSAYISTS
AND WORDSMITHS ...

LANDFALL ESSAY COMPETITION 2018

PRIZE: $3000 CASH AND A YEAR'S SUBSCRIPTION TO *LANDFALL*

RECENT WINNERS

LAURENCE FEARNLEY ┊ ALIE BENGE ┊ AIRINI BEAUTRAIS ┊ TRACEY SLAUGHTER ┊ DIANA BRIDGE ┊ TIM CORBALLIS

ENTRIES CLOSE 31 JULY 2018

RESULTS WILL BE ANNOUNCED IN LANDFALL 236, NOVEMBER 2018

www.otago.ac.nz/press/landfall/awards/otago065482.html

the mine wife

*

most nights
I just o.d. on tv,
sit there in a headwind
of static. With you around
I might have baled
the washing, picked up
the knucklebones of toys. But
I'm the wrong make
for taking this
on alone. I stare
at the mess, then flag it.
So what if flies are left
doing fieldwork
on plates I can't see
the point scraping
off—a.m. the tv's a holding
pen for people
who know the pain
of old news.

*

that first day our hands went south
like we picked up messages from trees—their leaves
were coming unlatched, but bare life didn't bother them.
They built a place we could lay down
rough & solid as a hallway: doubt was not
visible from there, only crossbeams
of sky, birds wiring together

the light. I'd held you off for long
enough, never one for unconditional
love songs: but my ribs felt
better in your fingers' scaffolding,
your hands honeycombed
with hard work.

It is always the moment
you can never have
back.

★

lights out,
what ends up on our bed
is only a body
that wants to harbour you.

There's no point to me now,
coming up
for air.

★

they'd be dog days
except that the kennels
are empty. I gave
the mongrels away. You know
the upkeep, & by day
two the barking
was under my chest
wall. Your mate
cleared them out for me:
they were broadside
with joy at making it
out the cage & on the bed
of the ute as he backed out they

had no traction.
That's happiness
for you.

*

some nightshifts you're still
in hearing. The corners
of the room smell
like your home
coming, your coat of
silt. Soft as you can,
you stomp off your steel
toes, & bulldoze into
bed—your creeping
was always an ambush.

Outside the birds
don't stop on my account.
I can feel your clumsy trunk
keeping its secret.
Like you, I hold my
breath.

*

There are worse things.
But some days I can't even like
the kids, their thick hands
tabby with dirt,
their naps shucked
with sandpit. As a mum
I'm getting close
to a write-off—you were the one
good at this. You'd
be lapping up their
numpty talk, the way

they chat through
spoons in dumb bubbles.
Lullaby & scuffle
would spread through
our lounge, till you tackled
them to bed. But now
I just want to be let
off the hook
for one fucking meal. It takes
me years to get past
their bedtime, their rooms
airtight with the last bloodthirsty
shush.

*

now I've lost you
they've invested in listening
to the earth. Out where
they brokered the hole, they run all
the tests they paid for with
your breath. Lover, you're dead on
bankable land. 29% was the rate
of return the company sent you in for—
I don't know if they've noticed it matches
the bodycount. But I know the word *return*
doesn't mean the same to them. They have
calculations—I have the fingernails
of dirt I wake with. All I know is today
they listed shares

in your open grave.

*

they had it wrong—that myth
where the bloke goes

down to the underworld
to haul her back. All I want
is the chance to dig,
one way. I'm not
asking to deadlift you
home. I'm over it, barefoot
& there's no deal
to be struck.

⋆

the night
you got on one knee
looking far-fetched, I needed
a fag, to mull. You could tell
I wasn't game, but you
still singled out a finger, spent
time trying to cuff
it with that flimsy
band that had set you back
weeks. Off & on, the stars
made a stopover. I shook off
my smoke & said *Nah*
& you just looked at me,
carved up. The light
on the trees
was cross-hatched & you
said *love* & I snapped
what's that when it's at
home then—though now
you won't get home I know

I'm in it
up to my eyes.

⋆

maybe I'll start
to have days when
I look from the outside
like I'm coping
all right. I'll bag
the kids' puzzles,
I'll trawl the floor
with buckets—yeah
that's it, I'll
hire a skip,
& strangle
the washing line
with ropey whites.
I'll tell the do-gooders
they can knock off
stocking the freezer,
the neighbours ganged up
on the doorstep
with casseroles: check it out
I'll tell them
I've already got
everything
spick
& dead

& span.

⋆

the sound of
the creek was once
blue-black & into my breastbone
you whispered a rundown
of our names. It was rush hour
in the trees. I practised my signature
on your trunk. Under us, all

the soil had was spare
time.

Once you were
a cleanskin

& the air
bottlenecked
in your kiss.

★

I don't remember
what makeshift
dress I'd yanked on or
how I'd rigged up my hair
the day we met, but I
know you were
chugging
a Coke & couldn't
stop gawking,
which was your hard luck.
The daggy fish & chip
shop chandelier
was decked out with
five p.m. flies, & in my
fist the docket
for a feed said eight of clubs.
I'd paid with shrapnel
the big kids packed in
a bread bag & swung
all the way to the shops.
On the telly over
the vats, the local
team choked, & everyone
looked clueless with

the heat.
I used to work
in a dump like this,
slapping the batter in
a yellow bucket,
then lowering
fish in the tub
with that foaming
clunk: that's the kind
of discount memory
the two of us got
talking about.
There was a fan
but it was hardly giving
the temperature
much flak. I
knew you were
already planning
long term
to go about touching me.
Out on the picnic
table where teens had
knifed the wood with names
they wanted to fuck,
those kids hoed in
& only left the rugged
scraps of batter
at the base of the nest.
But I didn't give two
hoots because afterwards
you leaned in
& scoffed
my lips like
you meant it.

*

the pinprick line
where your eyelids
seed each lash
is coloured
like roll your own.
I should still
have time to kill,
watching you shine
under there
while your dreams join
the dots.

*

the hand is a useless
surface for showing
the love it takes
to clear a path. Under
layers you wait for me to sift
your face from its mask.

*

to stand at the mouth
it takes a long journey. It's like
a cathedral to all
we've done wrong.

It's the peace
of the place that caves me in.

Those birds go on dialling
god. Even without you, the trees
don't come to a standstill. Healing is
not clear cut. Air makes the sound of where
you were last seen. I listen
for scraps in the hush.

The Age of Reason

Because longing
Because hormones
Because thirty-six
going on thirty-seven
Because psychotherapy
Because not understanding
Because antidepressants
Because New Zealand
Because domesticity
Because being scared
of enjoying domesticity
Because Simone de Beauvoir
Because money
Because *the best start*
Because not enough money
Because middle class
Because regret
Because my issues
Because potential regret
Because nieces and nephews
Because fear of death
Because a dog might do
Because antidepressants
Because déjà vu
Because the trees
Because the population
Because plastic
Because the ocean
Because everything
Because nothing
Because maybe
Because baby.

ALICE MILLER

Epilogue

I'm not here to repair the world.
No one here's here for much, except
perhaps these high windows boasting sky.
My friend says love is easier the less
you know a person. The more you know
the less you love. I say love's
an exhausted word, used for everything.
I turn the tap on, cold, the stream smooth,
and I can't remember why in Hell
I should turn it off.
Doesn't language get tired?
Doesn't it get sick of
lulling us into believing
all the **** we say? In the Prater a willow dips herself
into water and stirs her own image, and
in the lake her leaves refract, refuse to repair.
Isn't love also the kind of cruelty
you give to someone because you can't hold
all that cruelty in your own hands?
All I know's I'm overflowing.
All I know's I'm overflowing and I'm not sure
how much of me the world can hold.

WEN-JUENN LEE

A Love Letter to My Mother: A work in progress

My mother speaks to me in riddles.
this is how I've learnt to say
      have you eaten?[1]
        what's the weather like?[2]
in the pregnant silence over Skype
She reads Guo Xiaolu and Xinran during the day
fills her head with disillusionment and the diaspora
trauma and loss
but she forwards me chain emails on the dangers of microwaved water
brings homemade dumplings in Tupperware containers when she visits me
and squints at my unmade bed
She tells me there are too many Chinese in Auckland
      I do not know what to say
how do you tell your mother
      about internalised racism
when she has watched you
      tug   your monolids
      widen   your eyes
squeezed your body into a box of palatable Asianness?
She takes astronomy classes at night.
I do not ask her why she stargazes
what she looks for   in the oily darkness
we go to a poetry reading on migrant women
I do not tell her
I remember her crying on the plane
I do not tell her
I wrote *sacrifice* in my book
but I did not know where to begin.

1   I miss you
2   I love you

Before Swearing Off Sentimentality Forever

one last indulgence:

I was twenty-one
and desirable

enough that you took
the steps two by two

stood breathless
on the landing

pounding
at my door.

sheltered bay

for my sister

| the best we can offer is a sheltered bay | a darling harbour | before dawn |
fog-undone | Dad parking up | my brother and me | preparing crenulations,
pa, mana | with yellow 'n' red bucket 'n' spade | dividing the sea and the
sky | birth's about sorting out the light | there's a rough, squat Memorial
Wall at Caroline Bay | but it doesn't help much | it is granite-grey | it feels
like wet sandpaper | only the lost marbles of grandparents help | Amiens,
Passchendaele, Thiepval | they are magnets to three-year-old knees | we hop
the first full stops of a violent century | I remember the trip because memory
rips to stick | like Velcro and birth | setting trenches in the sea | revealing
red-emerge mornings | a scraped-knee day | the best we can offer is a
sheltered bay |

AIMEE-JANE ANDERSON-O'CONNOR

Lorne Street

The girls next door are *wild things*.

My sister and I found them one day stealing the loquats on our side of the chicken wire fence. We threw grapefruit overarm until they surrendered and brought us a fistful of honeysuckle. Their feet are black and their white shirts are grey. They dress like boys. Fringes choppy and full of grease. Their house is bigger than ours but the front door does not close all the way. There is a beat-up old Land Rover in the front yard with no doors or headrests or tyres. We pretend we can drive right down the train tracks on the metal rims. We are train robbers and we are conductors and we are squatters *and we'll shoot ya before ya can blink thank ya kindly.*

The kitchen windows are so grubby they look frosted. Dead flies hang, crossed feet, from the corners. The place smells cold and sweet. There is no couch but the girls draw chalk flowers on the walls. We sit on the floor and watch movies. We eat popcorn. My sister and I crack the unpopped kernels between our molars and hold them on our tongues. The other girls spit the shards at one another and they bounce right off their bent blonde hair. We make a stage out of beer crates and dresser drawers. We dance with wooden spoons and can openers. We wear holed socks on our hands and colanders on our heads. Throw jasmine rice at the adoring audience, sold-out stadium show. The grains nestle between the floorboards. We huddle under the table and slurp chicken noodles from the same pot. Buckled black at the centre, it rocks as we attack it with four gnarled forks.

Most of their toys are sharp and broken but they always have playdough. It is hard at the edges and gets stuck underneath our nails. It has glitter and can be everything all at once. Their father reminds them to share. He has a dark grey beard and wet kind eyes. He sits in the corner of his room and reads tattered crime novels. The room is lit Oz green through the beer bottle windowsill. He smokes bustling cigarettes and is quiet against our yabber.

Lavender incense curls into itself on the mantelpiece. The smoke twists up past a gold frame. A blonde woman with an autumn smile holds a bundle of white. Her glass is cleaned daily.

Their dad can make anything out of anything. He chops wood in the back yard. The axe glints and he whistles and our German Shepherd doesn't even blink. We pluck sweetcorn from their garden and eat it raw. It tastes like sunshine and dirt. He hacks raspberry jam into a handkerchief and the girls go quiet and my sister and I go home.

We bring over a basket of grapefruit and mandarins. Dad has baked fat scones and Mum cuts a blush of freesias.

My sister and I put in the best loquats.

We clamber over the chicken wire sag and hold hands.

The front door is sealed shut.

MARK EDGECOMBE

For Steve at 40

What I remember is you
overhead, phone out and held
before you by an arm

crooked Elizabethan-actor
style. I was weeding
alongside the stream

and you were reading *Les Fleurs
du Mal* in translation.
What was once in this town

only Rankine Brown's to offer
can now be summoned on buses,
trains, in cafés and cars

stopped on motorways,
and on the bridge that spans
the Takapu Stream:

Ze Floweurs of Evil.
What this valley would give
to be done with gorse and broom,

but you, you reading aloud
were another of those signs
from Kingdom come: work

made good by words in flower
like the scrub you declaimed them over.
Ton souvenir en moi luit comme un ostensoir!

from Fancy Dancing

ii.
Phaedra laughed when I told her what I was thinking.
'For god's sake,' she said, 'get over yourself
why don't you.' I'd picked her up near Lake Dunstan.
She was hitch-hiking to Roxburgh or maybe it was Clyde.
She was going to spend the summer picking fruit,
Moorpark apricots and black Dawson cherries.
The day was helluva hot. 'It's a serious business,'
I told her. 'We all want to die gracefully, don't we.'
'Not me,' she said, and she laughed again because
she was young and pushy. 'I'm going to live forever.'
What are we to do with the sufferings of this world?
Rinse them in the blood of The Lamb? The beautiful
Trappist's prayer was to go to the country
beyond words, where the trees are. It sounds like a plan.

The Girl Who Shaved the Moose

Grace got up early because they were going to the museum.

She got ready for school with time to spare. She didn't sprint for the bus. She stood at the end of her driveway, running her shoe through the gravel. She made wave patterns, circles. She picked up a handful of gravel and crunched it in her fingers. She stroked the gatepost, its fur of lichen.

They'd leave at playtime. The bell startled Grace out of a haze in which she was punching holes in a worksheet with the sharpened end of a pencil. 'Hand your sheets back in,' Mr Miles was saying, 'and stand behind your desks.'

Grace looked at her sheet, horrified. No one could read a word of it: it was a minefield. Grace wasn't angry, she just hadn't noticed she was doing it.

She pushed her worksheet to the bottom of the pile, walked back to her desk, stood next to her friend Joel. She stood still and quiet, shoulders set, back straight. Joel was wriggling.

'Anna, Riley, Paige, you may go to the bus,' Mr Miles said. Three goody-good girls left the room. Grace kept standing still. Joel kept wriggling. 'Fucken stop wriggling,' Grace hissed. Grace and Joel got on the bus last.

They sat behind Mr Miles, partly because he'd told them he'd be keeping an eye on them, but also because Grace liked to be near him. He was her favourite teacher ever. There was something very gentle about Mr Miles. He never yelled. When he didn't like your behaviour he'd give you a sad look. Mr Miles didn't smile an awful lot, but he always kept his cool.

'Mr Miles has a boyfriend!' someone yelled. It was Caleb.

Grace turned around. 'Shut up or I'll fucken punch you,' she said.

Grace watched Mr Miles's neck as it slowly swivelled. He had chosen to ignore Caleb. 'Grace,' he warned. But she could see in his face that he wasn't angry.

Mr Miles did have a boyfriend, but it wasn't any of Caleb's fucken business.

Grace heard a scuffle behind her. Caleb and Mason were fighting over something. They were a few seats back. Grace saw a glint of silver and perspex. She thought she knew what it was. But how had they got it?

Grace checked that Mr Miles was looking elsewhere, then dropped to her knees on the bus floor. The old lino was sticky and sandy. 'What are you doing?' Joel said, starting to laugh.

'Shut up,' said Grace. She was little. She could get under the seats. She went between her bag and Joel's, between the legs of Riley and Anna, who squealed, past Georgie and Charlie, and got to Caleb. She rose from under the seat with a fierce look. She fell on Caleb with all the force her small frame could summon. The surprise momentarily stunned him. She wrested the thing out of his hand, walked back up the aisle, stood beside Mr Miles's seat, and said, 'Here.'

Mr Miles looked into Grace's hand and saw his keyring, with his keys, and the tag with a photo of him and Grey on it. He looked into her face, half confused, half accusatory. 'Caleb had it,' she said.

Mr Miles stood up and leaned over the seats. 'Caleb, did you take my keyring?' he asked.

'No,' said Caleb, but Mason was giggling and shouting 'He did! He took it off your desk!' Caleb wrapped his hand over Mason's mouth, and a wrestling match ensued. Mr Miles looked helpless. 'Wait behind when we get off the bus,' he said. His voice sounded tired.

The man from the museum was teaching them about war. It was easy to get all the wars mixed up. The uniforms were dull. The guns looked like they had never been touched, you couldn't imagine the bayonets red. The photos of young men had faraway, dead looks in their eyes. They weren't dead when the photos were taken, but they were dead shortly afterwards. Or at least they were dead now. Maybe one or two might be alive, wetting their pants in wheelchairs. It was all very sad, but it was also very boring.

They walked upstairs to another part of the exhibition. Grace looked at the stair rail, how it curved around. It would be fun to slide down. Later, when everyone was doing their worksheets, she could try that. She hung back. The class gathered in a space between two glass cases. Grace stood at a distance from which she could hardly hear. It was better that way, because she was not listening.

She looked around her. There was an old carriage with a life-size black plastic horse harnessed to it. The harnesses were frozen solid. The horse felt eerily smooth, sounded hollow when she tapped it. On the wall behind her were some heads: a deer, some kind of antelope with long, squiggly horns, a moose with enormous craggy antlers. The moose was the best. A good part of its neck was attached, and it leaned out far into the room, as if it might bellow over all their heads. Closer, it smelled of cupboards, of fly-spray. Its fur was coated in a brittle haze. Fur-spray? It was not fresh fur. The moose had been dead over a hundred years. Its eyes were glass, looking at nothing. They reminded Grace of when the home-kill butcher shot the steers. Or when her dad brought back a rabbit from the paddocks, limp and dripping. The eyes open but not seeing. It was creepy.

Grace felt a small shock run through her arm as her hand touched something coarse. Her fingers pushed through the brown bristles. Under the fur, the moose's leather was dry and powdery. She looked at the whale skeleton hanging in the atrium. She heard Mr Miles's soft voice in the background, talking about medals. Grace was not interested in medals. The sound of his voice was comforting, though. So was the feel of the old dead fur around her fingers, as she worked her hand up and down the moose's neck. She reached up to touch its antlers, and saw that her hand was hairy.

Grace looked down at her palm with a thrill of horror. There was a hank of moose fur loose in it. Her fingers closed around it. It felt crunchy. Blood made a whooshing sound around her ears. Quite a lot of fur had come away, and there was a patch, not exactly a bald patch, but a patch of short brown hair, like a mouse's coat, left behind. The hole in the shaggy coat was like a burn, or a fungal infection. The moose looked even deader than it had before.

Grace stuffed the fur into her pocket, shuffled closer to the class. What were they meant to be doing now? They were going downstairs. She traipsed after them, back to the bag area. Mr Miles handed out clipboards, each with a worksheet. But she couldn't keep her hand out of her pocket, couldn't stop crumbling the fur through her fingers. Joel saw her. 'What's in your pocket?' he demanded.

'Nothing.'

'What's in your pocket?'

'Nothing.'

'I said, *what's in your pocket?*'

'Nothing.'

'Come on.'

'Moose fur.'

'Giz a look. Oh wow. I want some too. Where'd you get the moose fur, Grace?'

'Upstairs.'

'Show me!'

Grace's whole body tingled with panic as Joel ran up the stairs chanting 'Moose fur, moose fur, moose fur!'

'Stop, Joel!'

He came to the moose. Grace arrived alongside him, panting.

'I can see where you got it from, over here,' Joel said, and started pulling more hair away.

'No! Don't, Joel! Don't! We'll get banned from the museum.'

'So? I don't care if I'm banned from the museum.'

'Stop!' Grace reached up to pull Joel's hand away, and her own hand closed over the moose's neck again.

Grace and Joel stood there, methodically, systematically, stroking the moose. Until all along one side of its neck there was no fur left.

Grace felt sick. Both her pockets were stuffed full of fur. Both Joel's pockets were too. Joel was going to take his home and put some in a box that used to have chocolates in it, and give the rest to his little brother. Grace didn't know what to do. She couldn't go home like this. She couldn't even go back to school. Mr Miles would see in her face that she had stroked a moose and souvenired its coat.

She needed to pee. She left her clipboard and pencil on a table in the atrium and slunk off to the toilets. In the cubicle, the first thing she did was un-pocket the moose fur and shove it all into the sanitary bin. The little trapdoor fuzzed with brown hairs. It was sticky with something womanly and unknown. They'd had the period talk at school, boys had twirled tampons around their heads and held them under taps and thrown them across the playground. Someone had stuck a pad to the back of Paige's jersey. Grace didn't know what it would be like, to have blood coming out of there. She was both afraid of, and excited by, the prospect.

It was quiet and safe for a few moments. Then someone came in, banging doors, ripping out paper towels and casting them across the floor. Grace felt everything dry up. I'll wait till she's gone, she thought. She waited. The noise continued. Mr Miles is going to notice I've been in here ages, she thought. What was worse—peeing within someone's hearing, or getting told off for lurking?

Grace slid open the lock, walked out gingerly. It was Jenna, twice her natural size in a black down jacket. 'You were in there ages,' Jenna said, not looking at Grace directly. 'You constipated or something?'

Grace turned furious red and went to the washbasin, turned the tap on. Jenna edged up beside her. There was a cake of soap in a tray. It was off-white and where it had dried and cracked were deep grooves of dirt. 'Lick the soap or you love Cameron,' said Jenna.

Cameron dribbled. He wore the same trackpants all week. He lived on a dairy farm and came to school with cowshit on his clothes. No one could love Cameron, probably not even his mother.

'Oh, yuck,' said Grace.

Jenna slunk her arm around Grace's neck, pushed her down to the sink. '*Lick* the *soap*,' she said.

There was nothing Grace could do. She licked the soap.

When Mr Finch walked in and said 'Somebody', you knew you'd have to dig your fingernails into your palms or you'd crack up. You knew you'd have to concentrate on not going red, because if you did, he'd think it was you. 'Somebody has been *wetting* little clumps of toilet paper and *throwing* them at the ceiling.' You'd start to shake, maybe a snort would escape your nose. Or worse: '*Somebody* has done a number *two* in the boys' *urinal*!'

'Somebody,' said Mr Finch, 'has compromised our school's reputation on the trip to the museum yesterday.' Grace felt a hotness filling her chest, spreading up through her neck, down her arms. Mr Finch knew. 'We have had a long and positive relationship with the museum,' he went on, 'but I'm not sure if we'll be welcome back after yesterday.' He paused, and looked around the cluster of faces, searching each one for a twitch of muscle, a blush of guilt. No one moved. 'Because *somebody*,' he went on, 'or some of *you*, took it into their heads that it would be a good idea to *shave* the fur off a *moose*.'

Around the room there were stirrings of mirth. Grace didn't feel like laughing this time. It was more that she was pinching herself so she didn't cry. She and Joel had agreed not to say anything, but what if he did? Joel was a blurter. And they hadn't shaved it! Why did Mr Finch think they'd shaved it? Grace thought of her mum's razors, pink and stubbly on the rim of the bath. She remembered the time she'd shaved her arms, out of curiosity, cutting painful nicks in her skin. Why would anyone want to shave anything? She would leave it all to grow. Every time she looked between her legs it was furrier there. It was comforting. Why would anyone bring a razor to the museum?

Mr Finch's glare panned across the room. Everyone was quiet, except Riley, who hiccupped, almost a laugh. Grace's whole body felt like it was filled with poison. She would be told off in front of everyone. Her parents would have to come in. She'd have to replace the moose. Where would you even get a moose from? Were there any mooses in New Zealand? Did a moose live in the open, or deep in the forest? Were mooses dangerous? Grace imagined being tossed high in the air on those big, blunt antlers, or pressed against a rock by an angry bull moose.

'I see,' said Mr Finch, still staring. 'No one is going to own up. In that case, the whole class will be held responsible.'

A groan rippled around the room. The children imagined hours of detention, watching the light through the stained classroom curtains getting dimmer and greyer as they stayed writing lines. What moved in a school after dark? Late for gymnastics. Missing out on games. Getting out of setting the table, but detention was worse.

'You will each write a letter this lunchtime,' Mr Finch said. 'You will apologise for damaging a museum exhibit. And you will promise to be sensible visitors in the future.' He nodded to Mr Miles, folded his hands behind him, and walked out.

Was that all? 'When you have finished your letter,' said Mr Miles, 'you may go to lunch. Use a clean sheet of refill. Remember how to do letter layout.' Mr Miles picked out his favourite blue whiteboard marker from the little tray underneath the board, and neatly wrote a prompt across the clean white space. That was another good thing about Mr Miles. His stuff was always nice. His board was never smeary.

Across the table, Anna and Riley were writing in glitter ink. Anna drew a picture of herself and a picture of a penguin. Joel's head was close to the desk and he was breathing hard. Joel hated writing. Grace looked at the blank paper and her stomach twisted. She felt in her pencil tin for her compass, touched the sharp point, concentrated on working on her desk hole. She poked it a little more each day. She was nearly right through.

One by one the students took their letters up to Mr Miles's desk. Mr Miles was eating a sandwich, and looked uncomfortable. Grace understood he was missing his lunchtime too. But what could she say? I am very sorry, it was me who shaved the moose. But not with a razor. Just with my hand. I am sorry. I love the museum.

Joel pushed his chair in with a loud smack. 'See you at the stump,' he said, walking away. Grace and Joel always ate their lunch on top of the stump. It was fun to pull off bits of bark, look for bugs underneath. Joel said if he found a huhu grub he'd eat it. Was he going to say anything? Would he own up? If he didn't, should she? Then it would all be her. She would get in all the trouble.

It was only Grace and the teacher in the room now. 'How are you getting on there, Grace?' Mr Miles asked, sounding tired again.

'Nearly done,' Grace said. Quickly and messily, she copied down the prompts. She added 'I am very sorry about the moose.' That was honest. She drew a moose head with a big smile, front on, antlers wide. She coloured it brown. She lifted the piece of paper off her desk, walked across the carpet.

'Here,' she said, sliding her letter into the middle of the pile.

'Thanks, Grace.' Mr Miles was looking at the clock. Grace stood there.

'Um,' she said.

'And Grace.'

'Yes?'

'About my keyring. Thank you.'

'Oh. That's okay.'

'I'd have had a hard time starting my car without my keys.' Mr Miles smiled a forced smile. He looked like he wanted to start his car and drive a million miles away, and never drive back.

'But no swearing next time, okay?'

'Okay.'

'And don't be too rough on those boys. You might hurt them.' It was a real smile now. Grace thought about this. She was smaller, but she was a good fighter.

Quietly, she said, 'It was me.'

'Sorry?'

'It was me who stroked the moose. I didn't mean to, but its fur came off in my hand.'

'You didn't mean to stroke it?'

'No. I mean, not really, but ...'

The real smile again. 'It must have been a pretty good stroke.'

'Mr Miles?'

'Yes, Grace.'

'How much detentions will I have?'

'No detention.'

Was this real? 'But it was me.'

Mr Miles was lifting his satchel, about to sling it over his shoulder. It was a soft black leather. 'I believe you,' he said, 'but I can't prove it.'

'So am I in trouble?'

'Yes.'

'So can I ever go back to the museum?'

'Yes. Grace, I have to meet a friend. Go have your lunch.'

Grace watched him slide in his chair, stared at him. 'Go have your lunch,' he repeated. 'I'm locking up in 5 ... 4 ... 3 ... 2 ...'

Grace ran to the door. The carpet was air. She felt ... She didn't know what she felt. She jerked the zip of her backpack, closed her hand around her drink bottle, dragged out the bread bag with her lunch in it. The playground was full of screams. The sky was a painful white.

BRENT KININMONT

The Companion to Volcanology

Along the dewy forest floor I am marshalled
by the soft batons of harmless snakes she said patrol

the undergrowth. I told her my own land
is sealed; when something far-fetched did slip through

it mated only with the heavy mooring rope it was
famously pictured wrapped around. Small wonder

I recoil, pull my ankle socks higher, when a striped
cord abruptly follows the slight trail of itself

back into the bushes. But for the companion she carries,
she won't pause. The gray slopes above the timberline

are still half the morning away. She says I'll gladly find
no more coverage there. Just crooked fingers of

melting snow, and steam from another hissing
caldera she has been aching to see.

What Dropped?

Egghorns! she cried.
What newborn rhinos might make

after puncturing their shells.
Early practice for all

the clashes to come.
But now things have settled

a children's page says rhinos don't
start out with horns.

They aren't even hatched.
As unlikely, in fact,

as eggs with appendages.
Just *acorns* all along, rolling

off an oak dresser
when the quake didn't stop.

Given

The French say
there is always a kisser
and one who is kissed. I don't know
if this is true, or even if
the French say it.

But it feels true, right, like
there is always the Earth
and the moon, a dog
and its owner, a gift
and the receipt, a cancer
and its victim, a sentence
and its full stop.

CHARLES OLSEN

The Merry Peasant

Formal and elegant she sat upright towering over me. A vigilant eagle ready to claw back Schumann's chords from infernal dissonance. Long silky hair shrouded her piercing eyes while mine were transfixed on the *f* encircled in pencil below a middle C; the staccato ants twitching—*frisch und munter*—fresh and lively.

All week I'd been the merry peasant who climbed trees and swung around on the rotary clothesline but here I crouched like a downy chick on the edge of the nest. Her words were less a squawk than a sad confirmation in my heart, 'You don't want to be here, do you.'

Eighty-eight still hammers and—*pianissimo*—tears descending my cheeks.

Kind Rush

It was late afternoon the following day when Michael and Kiki emerged from Boca's. The same car was still parked in the loading zone outside Verona. They wandered up K Road towards Ponsonby. A swirling pattern of grey and yellow tiles on the footpath leapt out like a collection of 3D squares. All around, a swell of fast, clean people walked past, clutching leather bags, wrapped in heavy coats against the wind.

Michael recognised some of the knowing stares they got from passers-by; the looks were piteous but full of morbid fascination. Thoughts formed and scattered in all directions, like dry leaves in the wind.

'Where did you say you work again?' he asked, trying to bring himself to ground. 'Sorry if I've already asked you this.'

'Cross Street,' she replied.

Kiki was quiet for a while, haughty and withdrawn.

'You're not from here, are you?' she said finally.

'Nah. Both my parents are. But they left before we were born.'

'So what're you doing here?'

'Mum moved back from Perth when I was kid,' he said without thinking, 'but I only came over about four years ago.'

Kiki stopped walking and turned to him. She raised one eyebrow in that tough way of hers but didn't persist. He didn't even know why he was telling her. It wasn't something he wanted to talk about. She accepted his silence and they kept on. Kiki was glorious with long peroxide-blonde hair and a beautiful collection of tattoos spiralling across her chest. Her face was painted with hard-lined makeup and she careened along K Road with complete ease. Like she owned it. She was a lioness, Queen of the jungle. Kiki stopped and stood against a brick wall layered with old posters, lit a cigarette. Her white hair flew Medusa-like around her face in the wind.

'So what are you doing tonight?' she asked.

'Not sure. I've got a few dramas at the moment.'

'Yeah?' She looked curious and passed him a lighter.

'I'm kind of living in my car. Got no cash until Tuesday. Just that kind of thing.'

Kiki grabbed his hand and charged up the street.

A decaying line of red brick apartments shifted unsteadily above them. Grey-silver sky pressed down over each peaked roof. A rusted white fire escape extended from the middle apartment down towards the awning of a dairy. Paint flaked off the window frames and a thin, makeshift curtain blew in the wind.

Kiki stood under the arch of a streetlight. 'Want to come up?'

In his state of bewilderment Michael was grateful for her decisiveness. She led him to the back of the building and up some metal stairs. They walked into a dark, narrow living area with a stencil painting of a naked girl in a garden of flowers. It was unframed, the canvas pinned to the raw brick wall.

Her bedroom faced K Road through windows he'd seen from the street. Kiki drew the curtains. Michael sat on the end of her bed and lowered his head between his thighs. He was coming down hard now; his body felt light and weightless as if he was disintegrating. A restless internal panic rose. He lifted his head and propped his elbows on his legs.

'I'm not feeling so great.'

Kiki sat next to him on the bed, unzipped her white high-tops and threw them into the corner of the room.

'I'm holding,' she said. 'Don't worry, I'll take care of you.'

She got up, rummaged through her shoulder bag and returned with a small black case. Michael lifted his head, saw her unzip the case and pull out two clean needles sealed in white plastic. He hadn't used a needle before—he told her that, with closed eyes. He wasn't immunised as a child. He'd never even felt that kind of benign violation: his mother and father chose to exist outside the mainstream in relation to most things.

A thin thread of resistance revealed itself, but he knew he'd surrendered long ago. He reached for Kiki, blind and needing her strength, begging her tenderness. She cradled his head in her hands and helped him lie flat on the bed. The paint on the ceiling rose peeled off in thin strips.

'It's a kind rush,' she said in a soft voice, lying down on the pillow next to him.

God, he wanted that. It sounded almost healing.

He didn't stir when Kiki walked off to prepare his hit. From the bed he heard the sound of water being poured, metal against glass, the plastic packet of the needle rip. The room was frightening and empty without her in it. Then he heard her footsteps across the old wooden floorboards, returning from wherever she'd been—the bathroom, he imagined. He sensed her presence above him. She laid his left arm over a pillow and gripped the top of his forearm with a hard, cold hand. The blood flow constricted, pushing towards the vein at his elbow. Kiki released her hand and flicked his vein with her finger. He flinched when she drove the needle in, not expecting that depth of penetration. Cool liquid entered his bloodstream and he was gone, swimming in long, elegant strokes through the clearest water.

The front doorbell rang and Michael bounced up the hallway to answer it. Daylight shone through flowers of stained glass. In his hand he carried a silver figurine of a man holding a sword. He placed the figurine in the pocket of his board-shorts and reached for the brass door handle. The heat of the day rushed at him, forty degrees at least. A tall Indian man he'd never seen before stood on the veranda and told him he'd come for the cat.

Michael looked towards the cane chair where Pepper usually slept, but it was empty. He told the man he'd get his mother and wandered back down the hallway. Michael liked the languid pace of Saturdays. He could still feel the gritty residue of salt water tightening across his skin.

When he got back to his bedroom he pulled the heavy brocade curtain aside and opened the window, flattening his body against the glass. He watched the Indian man walk out the gate with a box. Heard the sound of his cat's cries, her claws scratching against cardboard, and then his mother's footsteps returning down the hall. The metal figurine pressed sharply into his thigh.

He found his mother on the sofa under the living-room window. A pair of rosellas shifted around in the eucalyptus near the tree-house outside. Michael sat next to her and asked why the cat had gone. Was she sick? The slack skin on his mother's jaw quivered as she explained in an erased voice that she had decided to sell Kimberly Street and leave Perth.

'Leo and you will stay,' she said.

His mother looked pained but her eyes remained distant and unyielding. He cried and begged her not to go, clung to her shoulders with desperate hands.

She held him, but her body felt stiff and motionless. In the end nothing he did or said made any difference. He was eight years old.

Michael pulled the door closed and began to run, holding Kiki's hand, across the street to his parked car. Rain slammed against the windows. His breath came fast. He looked back at the house they'd just come from, then over at Kiki. She sat next to him in the passenger seat, water dripping off her hair.

'That was mental,' he said.

Apart from the high-spec security it was just like any other house in Newton. His jaw ached; he'd been clenching it so long. A blend of music, loud voices and barking dogs made its way into the car from across the street. He listened with a growing sense of disquiet.

'Where am I taking you now?' he asked her.

Kiki seemed different. Without making eye contact she told him to take her to Cross Street. It occurred to Michael then that he was messing around with a gang girl. The implications of this looped around in his head. Maybe she had a guy? He saw himself in a range of violent scenarios. He looked over at her again, trying to gauge his safety. But she appeared indurate and blank. He wished she'd laugh or say something, anything to break through his impending doom.

On Cross Street he pulled into an empty carpark a way back from an ominous building with blacked-out windows. Vixen. He'd heard about this place. Old steel walkways ran above them, connecting a carpark to the Iron Bank building—an enormous stack of concrete, steel and rust. Frenzied coloured light leapt across the dashboard. Kiki sat beside him blowing smoke out the open window.

'I had fun hanging out with you,' she said, flicking her butt and gathering her things into a large shoulder bag. She stayed seated for a while, as though she was waiting for something.

'You do know about Boca, hey?' she asked, turning to look at him. Lights from the dashboard danced across her beautiful face, and the indicator he'd left on kept ticking.

'What the fuck?' he replied.

She shook her head and laughed, almost to herself, then stepped out onto the street. Michael watched Kiki's figure recede into the gloom. A large spotlight sat on the top of the club she entered, waiting to illuminate the arcane world beneath it. Somewhere, not far away, he heard the sound of glass smashing, the crush of aluminium. Michael stayed in the car, staring into the black, and experienced a sensation like falling.

An image flashed before his eyes. Waking on Boca's bed—had it been day or night? Boca standing over him, jeans around his thighs, cock in his hand, pumping hard. Face contorted, yellow teeth grinding in his beak-like mouth. Get away, man. Get away, he'd said. Was that a dream? Was that real? He couldn't be sure.

The indicator was still on. Its relentless ticking hammered through his head like a pick-axe. He reached for the lever and flicked it off. Got out of the car and headed towards a 24-hour bottle shop.

When he walked in, the guy at the cash register glanced up, then went back to his phone. Michael wandered through the red wine section and managed to slip two bottles under his raincoat, securing them in the elastic waist of his shorts. He walked back to the register and bought a packet of cigarettes with twenty dollars Kiki had given him. He carried the wine back to his car and decided that he should move on.

When Michael regained consciousness he was slumped in his car outside Achilles House. The sun was just starting to rise across the damp bonnet. He pushed back against the driver's seat and closed his eyes. His feet were bare. His brain felt juiced.

He turned around, scanning the back of the car for his missing shoes. It appeared they were gone. Without success he tried to recall what had happened to them, but it no longer seemed important. The inside of his mouth was thick and dry. He ran his tongue across the blisters on the insides of his cheeks. Outside the car, good humans were starting to make their way through the city with takeaway cups of coffee.

In front of the car, three red witches' hats stood in a solid triangle around a construction sign that said Work Ends. The car glovebox was open and the blade of his fish-filleting knife flashed in the morning sun.

Michael staggered out of the car, heart pounding in his chest. He fell against the door and sprawled back, staring down Customs Street, trying to get his bearings.

The American Embassy building towered over him. A Stars and Stripes flag waved in the breeze and square mirrored windows reflected a fast-moving sky. All the conflicting lines of the city began to pulse. They warped into distorted, frightening shapes like melted plastic. A strobe light started off in his head, alternating chaotically between sound and image.

The table was set for the evening meal. Laid with white china, wine glasses and a vase of flowers. The white and pink lilies exploded into too-bright stars. Sticky orange dust from the stamens fell onto the tablecloth. Michael picked up his fork and tried to ignore his father.

'Your mother is a bitch,' he ranted. 'She abandoned you. Do you not understand that? I'll never forgive her.'

This happened whenever his father had been drinking. Yellow liquid sloshed around the bowl of the wineglass in his hand. Thin lips curled around glass. His father reached across the table and poked Leo's elbow with the tip of his knife.

'Get your elbows off the table,' he barked at Leo.

Michael imagined stabbing him in the eye.

His father peered down at them. 'What kind of woman does that?' he asked, grey eyes diluted and watery, as if he might cry.

Michael looked at Alison, his father's girlfriend, to see if she'd do anything but her mouth was pursed like a cat's bum. Her smug silence said she was enjoying this. Alison was younger than his mother. She wore makeup, applied with brushes and sponges from shiny blue-and-gold compacts.

He kicked Leo under the table and his brother raised his big, gentle eyes. Leo knew the order of things. Michael zoned his father's words out and thought instead of the photo he had of his mother buried in his top drawer. He held the image in his mind and counted in his head to a hundred.

His bare feet appeared pale and grotesque on the black bitumen. The American flag still billowed in the wind. The acute loneliness of those first years without his mother returned. The nights were the worst. When Michael missed her so much that his chest ached and burned. There was also the terror of dreaming. Of being lost in a vast city and catching glimpses of her between tall buildings before she was absorbed and swallowed by a giant metropolis, and him alone, wandering in panicked circles through a maze of busy streets, endlessly searching her out.

The nerve endings snaking across his scalp were on fire. Michael called out and clawed at his head. People on the street looked up, then kept on. He turned around and fell back against the side of the car, bringing his forehead down against the dewy blue metal. Loss was all that life had shown him. His mother, his brother, his sister—where were his people now? It made no sense the way the world spun. It was ruthless and arbitrary in its justice. He staggered around the car, circling its perimeter, and reached through the window into the glovebox for the knife.

He walked towards the post office on the other side of the road. A woman with dark short hair cut in front of him and he followed her blindly. She bent to open a red box. Michael stood behind her and showed her the blade of the knife, muttering something unintelligible in a strange guttural voice. The woman whimpered and offered him her handbag.

Cool leather touched his fingertips and a veil lifted. Real light shone on the knife in his hand. The unknown features of a middle-aged woman stared back at him in terror. Michael dropped the knife and ran towards the waterfront.

CHARLOTTE SIMMONDS

Irresponsible Late-night Splenetic

Every night in my dreams I see you, I feel you,
mostly because the last thing I do before going to bed
is read the news, the first thing I do on waking up.

You know how people are afraid of things they don't understand
and some people try not to think about the things they are afraid of
but me I try to understand those things because maybe then

I will be less afraid. So I read the news eight times a day,
last thing before going to bed, first thing on waking up,
and I know sane people might advise me to stop reading the news

but it's not the news that makes me anxious, it's the news
that helps me unwind, and with the late-night shows now, instead
of being anxious, it's all a bit of a panto and I think every day,

Oh yay, you're cocking even more crud up, now you will be
easier to impeach, the more crud you cock up the less likely
you are to stay the full term, oh yay, hooray, goody, goody

gumdrops. Actually I don't see you or feel you every night
in my dreams. I sleep really well, I don't see you or feel you
at all. Reading the news relaxes me, takes the edge off of

life. Now I am calm enough to go to sleep and see other people,
feel other people, read other people, grab other people by their
semi-colons and commas. Every night in my dreams I see

books and feel books. Every night in my dreams I wander
around chit-chatting with my mates. Everyone wants politically
engaged poetry these days. They want responsible art,

art that is accountable and an accountant and an auditor,
they want stuff that says something and means something
and does something. But I just read the news and go to

sleep. I'm out of fashion, out of touch. I don't have anything
to say that isn't being said better on Twitter, that isn't already
in the *Guardian*, and both the late-night Jimmys are much

better looking than me. All I'm trying to do is not move
too much so the ruptured spleen will continue its slow
moving loss of blood and not burst forth into rapid

internal haemorrhaging, sending me into hypovolemic
shock. If the blood leaks out slowly you can repair it,
but if it is fast you can't clean it up in time. You can't

stop all the leaks. The spleen is a red and white house,
it is part of the lymphatic system, it grants you a lot of
immunity. There is a large number of macrophages, those

holding cells that eat up the other ones when they've
stopped doing their job, they destroy them, wipe them out,
lay them to waste. When the spleen is working correctly,

that is. When it isn't damaged or ruptured. Even a little
bit of damage can cause a rupture later on. And even a rupture
can let you go on living for weeks without showing any

signs. As long as it's slow you can cover it up. If it's slow,
your body can keep it from you, hide it, you might never
find out. Just don't make any sudden moves. Don't laugh,

don't cough, don't blow your nose, and above all don't
reach too high, don't stretch yourself, don't try to push
beyond your limits. Know your reach. Stay there. But

the signs of shock are unmistakable: pallor, cold clammy
hands, profuse sweating, anxiety, mental confusion, high
heart rate, high respiratory rate, low blood pressure and

when you click your nails, your fingers don't go white then
red. But don't worry about that, that only happens once you've
lost at least 20% of your blood volume. You're miles away

still. You've still got 38% popularity. You're in the clear.

Artificial Cold, Genuine Heat

Despite the dark, it was immediately clear to Ronnie that fridges were never designed for viewing from below. Underneath there is no soft plastic whiteness with the 'attractive bevelled edges' advertised. Only metal turned rust, gone harsh and bubbled and ugly.

An incongruous warmth surrounded him and the scent of dirty ice clung to each breath. Stagnant water retains its stagnation once frozen, he supposed. His heart struck the ribcage as if it were planning to burst from his body and escape. Yet a flange pinned Ronnie's elbow to his chest and left no egress for the organ, regardless of how he lay.

Twisting and thrusting, Ronnie attempted to push his top half out from the sinkhole, but found it proved difficult with both arms forced into pretzel shapes. He could touch his face and throat with one hand, and curl the other under the fridge's side—but he was otherwise bound from the waist up.

With feet flat to the ground, Ronnie raised his hips in the air and rolled his shoulders in their ivory sockets. As if his shoulders were replacement legs, he shifted his weight from one to the other in the inverted crawl of some extinct insect. The fridge shuddered with each motion, until it took one timid step. Even in the dim, he could see the small triangular feet of the fridge nearing the edge of the crater. If a single leg dropped, he would be truly and unceremoniously crushed.

'Help,' he uttered, without certainty.

No answer came, save the uncrinkling of a plastic bag he had left on the bench.

'Help! I'm under the fridge!' he yelled.

In this little enclosure the resonating sound of his own voice seemed performative and uncanny.

Reminiscing back to mere minutes ago, he could not now make sense of why he had gone beneath in the first place. Alarm, most likely. The earthquake was not strong enough to knock anything over, but somehow it had ruptured the linoleum, leaving a sizeable hollow beneath the unshaking fridge. At that moment he had felt the need for an inspection of the sinkhole in case a pipe had burst—but he hadn't even grabbed any tools before he contorted into a shape that could fit. Odd how instinct can work.

Now he simply lay, letting images of cross-sections come to mind. The fridge with its shelves and foods and milks; the freezer, with contents obscured by ice; then himself. Ronnie, bent into the shape of a musical note on its side, his body following the angles of the hole in the earth.

Ronnie considered calling out again, but such a trifling earthquake wouldn't occasion an emergency response team or anything. But Felicity, his flatmate, was only at the supermarket so he wouldn't remain unaided for long. How many people are trapped like this each day? How few ever get out? With the hand closest to his face he touched the warm metal and tried to find an edge.

Imagery of an action-hero escape materialised within and he saw himself tugging at the metal, tearing out screws and electric cables with his bare hands. Disembowelling the fridge from below. His skin would split as he wrenched the plastic apart, allowing all the frozen peas and pizza bases and ice to spill into the hole with him. Then he would drag his legs into the sinkhole too, punching open the freezer door and emerging with frost on his eyelids and freedom in his grip. But Ronnie could not find an edge to curl his fingers around. Instead, he lay.

As his heart rate began to slow, something fell from the metal above and landed on his forehead. He blinked rapidly in surprise and pulled a face. Another drip of cold water fell, landing in the same spot. The water was probably swimming with diseases and microscopic creeps carrying filth on their backs. He once read an article online about defrosted ice, detailing how restaurants used toilet water to make ice cubes, and then refroze melted ice cubes to sell again. Ronnie was glad the fridge water did not fall near his mouth.

'Can anyone hear me?' he asked softly, hope long gone.

Again the drip hit his head. Over and over in the same spot. They tortured people like this, didn't they? With time it feels like a drill to the skull. As if the water burrowed deeper with each following droplet until it was inside the skin, the bone, the brain. His drip fell at a consistent pace, and he couldn't remember if that was what drove you insane, or whether it was the inconsistent intervals.

The incessant drips formed a small wet puddle behind his head and he began to think about death. You must feel waterlogged when you die. A few years back he had fallen from a tall tree and landed on his neck. Much of the detail was gone, but he remembered how it didn't really hurt but his spine felt all wet—just like it did now. What are we but vessels? Grecian bladders carrying essential wine, only to be disposed of when we're empty of that which kept us alive. Juice boxes. The fridge sputtered in support of the concept.

Ronnie calmed himself and tried to lie as still as he could, his asthmatic wheezes identical to the voice of swans. Somehow the rubble under his back had formed around his shape and felt strangely comfortable, although he wouldn't admit it if you asked. He looked up to the metal above, really looked. Tried his hardest to see. The limited light that reflected from the kitchen floor added an emphasis to the texture and he could feel the surface without even needing to stretch out his hands.

Something changed. Now he could see in the dimness as if all were lit, but could no longer smell the dirty ice or brown lettuce. Even the torturous drip slid down his face without effect. The bubbled metal was orange and grey, and directly overhead was an iron grille he had not realised existed until then. It was now that Ronnie understood, or at least recognised what he had always known. It was never fear he had been experiencing. As if commanded, his eyelids pulled together and the drip dripped.

Still far from certain, he began to accept that it was something closer to pleasure that followed the ridges of his spine. Maybe it was the discovery of a new fetish, like those people who get off from being vacuum-packed or swallowed by quicksand. There was some inconsequential, half-repressed desire to remove his clothing and embrace the ambiguous cold-warm tension of the metal—but it was not titillation.

He felt no sexual excitement or sensual overload, but something closer to the satisfied dullness after the act. The post-coital stupor, that pure solipsism where all the senses have been so overwhelmed that all subsequent feeling is contradiction. Passionate indifference, blissful discomfort, prideful guilt.

Underneath, he was the only reality. There was no neighbourhood, no country, no earth—just Ronnie and the fridge. A philosophical blank spot which, as he cautiously opened his eyes, he found had returned with the perceived dark. Perhaps he amplified the darkness himself, pushing the light aside to better embrace the emptiness. People say that black is the absence of light, but there is no true absence if you get close enough. At the atomic level, it's all just reconfiguration and never removal. He knew to no longer force himself to see, only to bathe in the metronomic thoughts that entered him. Solitude, satisfaction, self-awareness. Drip drip drip.

There was an extended period in his life where the space beneath the bed provided him the same comfort. Whenever his parents fought, whenever the shouts floated between the walls he would lie there with nothing but the dust and the tightness for company. The sense of his own context fell away and he became a boy born surrounded by nothing, thus becoming everything. He felt those odd rumblings of feeling deep within himself then, too, but gave them no attention.

Earlier than that, he found that under that very same bed was his favourite spot for hide-and-seek. All his friends soon started to look there first, knowing how likely it was that he would be there. So instead, Ronnie hid between bedframe and mattress, completely engulfed on all sides and barely able to breathe. The first few times it was difficult not to giggle and reveal himself, but soon he would forget about the game entirely and just lie in the emptiness. His friends never once found him there.

What of his desire to pick out the heaviest blankets, the tightest clothes; his fear of open spaces; his distaste for being on top and not having his partner's frame pushing down on him? It could also be why he preferred sleeping with people who were heavier, taller than he was. All was explained to him. No wonder he couldn't resist the enticing slope that led to all-consuming tightness beneath. It was little less than destiny.

With a slight joyful shiver, Ronnie exhaled and began to run his fingertips across the metal so close to him. The imagined hole in his head had reached bone, but it wasn't too painful. Just new and wet. He stretched out his finger and rubbed the cold patch of unharmed skin. Even if his fingers couldn't find it, the hole remained. Pretty soon he would feel his brain spilling out. No matter.

The fridge's motor whirred and fluctuated in its aluminium cage, whispering secrets to him. A chittering, inconsistent voice of animalistic orgasm—showcasing emotion more impassioned than he was used to from his living peers. Can something both fascinate and repulse? He listened to the noise and tried to visualise the beast it could be coming from.

Tall and angular, with a gait equally imposing and vulnerable. Something enormous but fragile, good-hearted, willing to embrace and soothe all who come near. The beast shuddered, its vibrating song rising in intensity as the steady drip of saliva continued to fall upon his head. It was hungry for him, but knew better than to give in to desire. Ronnie stroked the creature, embraced it. Slid his fingertip into the faulty pipe and dabbed the water to each eyelid, indicating that he felt empathy for that impossible tender animal.

With unforeseen passion, he dragged his trapped arm across the rusted flange and felt blood hit his shirt. Once again, the fridge shifted ever so slightly and the pressure grew greater, warranting a soft moan. Both arms free, he slid them around each side of the fridge in a luminous embrace and pressed his cheek to its underside. Ronnie could remain below there for all his days with the beast, growing old and fat until the space grew even tighter. Such a selfless thing, it would surely tear a hole in itself and feed him the many succulent things that lay inside its very belly if only he stayed.

In the darkness, the timeline came to him in the form of another cross-section. There lay Ronnie over the years, his hair and nails growing forever, his limbs gradually atrophying, the drip of water passing through his entire skull and into the cement—all while the smile sat unwavering upon his lips. To be crushed is to be supported, he surmised.

Somewhere out in the infinite distance of the house, a door swung closed. Footsteps neared, and ever so slightly the light began to drain back in.

'Please don't,' Ronnie mumbled.

He clenched his eyes shut and shook his head back and forth, pushing closer to the rusted metal. Yet each resounding footstep on the linoleum brought distraction, a return to reality and a remove from the perfect isolation of the under-fridge.

It was Felicity, of course, and the light came back into being. With a dejected sigh, he closed his eyes and patted the fridge's side lovingly—planting a desperate, passionate kiss upon the grille overhead. Felicity dropped the groceries and shouted something in despair, but Ronnie was too busy bathing in his fridge's winter-warmth to hear what it was.

The Piano Girls

for Chris

Seven priests, Cecilia counted, but then Father Stephen stepped out from behind Monsignor Gerrard and there were eight. 'A goodly discretion,' her mother would have said, presuming they were all there for her. In the body of the old wooden church, whose timbers appeared to be swelling in the heat and the chocolate brown Gloria in Excelsis Deo on the proscenium melting, the congregation were fanning themselves with orders of service while Maria Szczepanski pushed and pummelled at the old harmonium. A single petal from a tired yellow rose fluttered down onto the sheet music of Jesu, Joy of Man's Desiring which no one could doubt Zuzanna Leadbetter would require at least twice.

And now Magdalena, the eldest sister, was on the stage, in front of the line of priests, announcing that she would not break her mother's ban on eulogies, but she simply wanted to congratulate the priests for being so many. Her mother, she said with only a slight tremor, would have wished to congratulate them as well.

There was a pause then, before the mass began. The full panoply, Cecilia thought, despite the heat. How many priests had her mother fed, how many families comforted by a casserole wrapped in a tea towel on a doorstep, how many children taken in, for rest and recuperation? Benevolent light ran down the undersides of her mother's arms, like the beam of a torch.

'Follow me,' she would say, calculating the bed linen, the turning of leftovers into a pie. And she would be thinking of a game for the children, something old-fashioned that might require parcels inside parcels, each shrinkage making the gift more treasured.

The first music recital was held on Zuzanna's birthday, August 17th, the year after her death. Her birthdays had always been special. There was never a guest list but the big farmhouse would fill with relatives and neighbours and strangers. On her sixtieth birthday a tramp was being passed from farm to farm for light duties like stacking wood. He sat at the kitchen table, blowing up balloons for a crowd of children. The sisters always made cakes—there was competitiveness between them. Cecilia's Victoria sandwich, Magdalena's red velvet cheesecake. Katharine, the youngest, who hated baking, would order something from the local bakery.

Cecilia and Katharine would slide onto the piano stool and play Happy Birthday as a duet with trills and runs and tempi that ranged from a slow foxtrot to a moody blues. Soon the guests would be dancing through the connecting doors, out into the hall to form a conga.

The old Calisia piano had always stood against an interior dining-room wall to shelter it from earthquakes and changes in temperature. There had been a number of earthquakes that summer: loud rumblings while the family assembled on the lawn. Inside the piano rocked sedately. Its dark mahogany and scuffed pedals, the metronome riding on its lid and sheet music spilling over from the stand or leaking from the stool like someone's unpaid bills. Katharine loved to run her eyes down the lines of staves, imagining someone like Carl Philipp Emanuel Bach quickly filling in the harmonies that were buzzing in his head and threatening to fly off. Or Wolfgang Amadeus Mozart, like a child doing his sums, bending over a sheet with Nannerl. How pedestrian their parents must have seemed to those two. Composition must have been like plucking stars.

Zuzanna Leadbetter had played her way through all manner of family crises: birth, illness, death. The sort of background worry that began each day: had the girls done their homework? Was it her turn for church flowers? Who to invite for Christmas now the tramp had moved on? It was paramount to face each day with optimism and the Calisia piano was always ready to suggest a Chopin mazurka or one of her favourite Goldberg Variations. She knew she was not a good pianist—her three daughters were far superior—but she took comfort in the way harmonies shifted, themes broadened just before the point of exhaustion, or a precipitando passage could be followed—as it was in her life—by a smorzando one. Sometimes, when she was particularly dissatisfied, she rose from the stool and banged down the lid.

Katharine and Cecilia had started playing duets when they were five and seven. They sat side by side, Wolfgang and Nannerl, while Magdalena (nine-and-a-half) turned the pages.

Sometimes she turned back too large a corner and a crucial note disappeared. Often they got down from the stool ready to hit one another. Already Magdalena had decided never to play a duet. Once she had witnessed a duet performed on two grand pianos; even the pianos looked like rivals. The pianists, in evening dress, were reflected in the shiny lids. Over the years Cecilia and Katharine played their way through Chopsticks, I Got Rhythm and West Side Story. But most of all they liked to improvise.

Just how Gus, Magdalena's husband, became part of the audience was never quite clear. It was the summer he was recovering from knee surgery, when his spirit, usually so organising and forward-looking, seemed to have suffered a setback. 'I'll stay in the dining room,' he promised, but when Magdalena was playing Poulenc's Novelette in C Major he crept out and sat on a pouffe his father-in-law had brought home from Egypt. If he caught anyone's eye he assumed a 'sick' expression at which, Magdalena realised, he was remarkably good.

A year later, Jeremy, Katharine's husband, followed. He had heard reports of a superlative afternoon tea. He could sit through Satie for that. After that it was a shoo-in for James, the only one among the husbands who really liked music. That he enjoyed Gilbert and Sullivan and Souza marches was irrelevant. He applauded the pleasure the Savoy operas had brought to so many stunted lives. At afternoon tea he tactfully helped himself to a slice of Cecilia's Turkish honey cake.

A bigger problem than the husbands who had inserted themselves like fugues was how to arrange the programme. How many items each? How long would their mother have liked to listen? She had never shown favouritism but each sister was regularly vouchsafed small signs. Katharine, limping along the hallway when Cecilia and Magdalena had run off, found herself swept into her mother's arms as she struggled with her crutches. (Her leg was broken and it was far from the adventure she had thought it was going to be.) Her mother, bulkier by the year, Katharine and a tangle of crutches ended up on the carpet together. Her mother held her there, uncomfortable but loved, in the circle of her soft arms. Then there was an almond biscuit from the big glass jar and cold milk in a thick green glass.

Magdalena had been all in favour of an overture to begin. Cecilia and Katharine disagreed. It was in the choice of music that conflict arose. Max

Bruch's Schwedischer Tanz in A Minor or Brahms' Hungarian Dance No. 5? 'Not Hungarian,' Magdalena insisted. 'Mother was Polish.' Should Chopin always be included? Katharine wanted to play Copeland: the bare essentials, a new way of thinking of her mother. A duet for the end or a trio? And tea was not to be laid until the final note.

Over the years—ten, coming up to eleven—Magdalena, Cecilia and Katharine had become more competitive. Cecilia walked up Magdalena's driveway and a cascade of notes drifted through the open window. Something with a lot of trills and a cracking pace. Magdalena hastily closed the lid. Cecilia practised a particularly difficult Liszt étude. She thought she would have disliked Liszt had she met him. She imagined he was a fanatic and modern women would throw their knickers at him. Once she had stayed in a coaching inn in Hebden Bridge and read a report of the rain and mud that had sabotaged the transporting of Liszt's piano. 'Liszt Stayed Here' was framed and displayed in the bar. She stood in the courtyard looking at the swift-flowing river with plastic bags pinned by boulders. This was the year she played Frog Puddles, which would surely have reduced Liszt to apoplexy.

Frog Puddles sandwiched between Mendelssohn (Katharine) and Beethoven (Magdalena). What a glare she got from them both as she vacated the piano stool. She bowed to the chair that held her mother's shawl.

'Loved that frog piece,' Gus said to her in the kitchen where he was refreshing himself from a hip flask. 'Got a bit of go to it.'

'You would too, if you were a frog,' Cecilia said.

One night she had followed a frog down the steps to her garden. The steps were wide and wet; there were puddles on each one. The frog, large and with good-size legs, took a hop for each step. Hop, pause. And Cecilia behind him, waiting as she waited for Katharine to count under her breath when they played a duet.

'Play that again and I'm calling the whole thing off,' Magdalena said when they were nursing bone china rose teacups that rattled in fingers with a slight tremor after Chopin. 'Otherwise we might as well turn it into a circus.'

'Mother liked circuses, if you remember. She ran the house like a circus. She was the ringmaster.'

'And you were one of the bare-backed ponies. Obedient to the core.'

Cecilia thought it was true. She liked the idea of light feet leaping from her back and re-landing, shaking the dust from her coat and sending flakes of skin, pony and human, into the air. Her hooves in the sawdust would be as sure-footed as Bach.

The following year's recital was the most ambitious ever. Mendelssohn's Duetto Op. 38, from Songs without Words; Kabalevsky's Sonatina Op. 13, the presto movement; the largo from Beethoven's Sonata in E flat. Gus and Jeremy took themselves off to the pub. They were rather inebriated when they returned to the last notes of Frank Bridge's Berceuse. 'Perhaps they will say a prayer,' Jeremy said. 'Or call in a priest.' Only Gus was Catholic, a Catholic who had long ago fallen out of his cradle. The other two had tried for a time, hoping to make business contacts, and then given up.

Secretly the husbands came to see if they had picked the right sister and usually their choices were confirmed. Magdalena whose vivacity came from a bottomless clear spring; Katharine, dreamy and introspective but saved by an unexpected wit that occasionally burst out. Cecilia, somewhere between the two, deeper and wilder, though she was never allowed to play Frog Puddles again. The carpet sweeper came out and Gus was handed a pair of rubber gloves and had an apron tied around his waist. Soon there were suds on the ends of his moustache. Someone mentioned dinner and there was a chorus of groans. They might order pizza. Or there could be something on at the movies.

'As long as it's not the life of Tchaikovsky or Beethoven,' James protested. 'I'm all musicked out.' Magdalena's marriage was in trouble and at the next recital Gus was absent. 'Ill-disposed,' Magdalena said, and the private meaning was just for herself. It was to herself that he was ill-disposed. Longer and longer silences, a withdrawal which, oddly, he was building block by silent block. She had begun to retreat herself, in equal increments. They might have been building a house together, working on opposite walls. Only, unlike real builders, they never looked at each other or sat companionably drinking tea. Cecilia and Katharine knew, of course. They couldn't play so much music together without knowing that music had its morals, no matter how skilfully they were concealed; usually the bass gave the game away. It was the reason Cecilia liked to play the bass in their duets while Katharine crossed her hands or lifted them daintily in the air, an affectation that Cecilia hated.

Yet like the underpinning bass, the marriage held. The flirtation that had promised so much, in Gus's opinion at least, died down. He was back in the tonal concealment of Mozart or Bach where a sleeve was more important than a heart. Magdalena would scoff, of course. Mozart was so secure he could gnash his teeth, weep, or laugh uproariously at a joke and no one would be the wiser. Slowly, they began talking a little more; they went to a nostalgic Italian film festival, watched Anita Ekberg wade in a fountain.

'What about a water theme?' Magdalena suggested when they were discussing the programme for the next recital. Debussy, obviously. Their mother had adored sea bathing. Everything sparkling and in motion.

'Nothing by Shostakovich,' she might say. 'I can't bear his unhappy life.' Chopin was sad too but that was put down to living with George Sand.

At home Katharine was practising for her LRSM. Jeremy had been made redundant and she thought she might take a few pupils after school. If she played one of her exam pieces at the recital no one would notice. It irked her that no one thought of her as a potential breadwinner. Her fingers struck the keys as they had when she was sitting Trinity Grade 4 at school. She had expected a haughty woman draped in scarves. Instead the examiner turned out to be a sandy-haired man in tweed. Glancing at him as she played Sweet Polly Oliver, Katharine saw that he had fallen asleep. At the final chord he suddenly woke and gave her a wide grin. When the results came out she had been awarded Distinction and on the examiner's report was a sentence addressed to her. 'Far from putting me to sleep as you imagined, your playing of "Sweet Polly Oliver" was one of the few occasions on this tour where someone truly entered into the spirit of the music.'

At night, before she fell asleep, Katharine replayed the scene in her head. She had had to cross a wide stretch of parquet floor on which her heels rang loudly. The room was ominously full of silence and the examiner had not looked up. To calm herself she imagined it was her father she was playing to; he, too, had listened to her playing with his full attention, never grimacing if she made a mistake or asking her to start again. When at last she lifted her fingers as if water drops were falling onto the keys, her father smiled to himself but was careful not to let her see. She came to him and nestled against his knee. 'Beautifully done,' he said, pushing back a tendril of her hair and, though it was a white lie, he told her Für Elise was his favourite piece of music.

No one, not even Zuzanna, knew how ill William Leadbetter was or that he had been visiting a cardiologist. He had kept the prognosis—a word that reminded him of an insect with feelers—to himself. 'There's no knowing with hearts,' the cardiologist had said. William had assumed his heart was in prime condition, like a Swiss watch. He thought of his three piano girls, taking turns at the old Calisia upright. Cecilia played to him while he had breakfast. Sometimes they were the only two left in the room and the breakfast table stayed uncleared while she stumbled through Bach's Minuet in G minor. From time to time the soft pedal flew up with a snap. 'A dangerous instrument, the piano,' he told her. He only wished he could forget the pain in his chest.

After his death—a mid-afternoon dash to the hospital, the operating theatre, Zuzanna waiting outside for the bearer of bad news (she could read the surgeon's face in a mini-second; even if it were not flushed she would have known)—it became obvious that their father was the centre of their family, not their mother as everyone assumed. Their mother let the garden go and four seasons came and went, adding leaves and twigs and wind. None of the children dared offer to help, recognising a symbol even if they could not name it.

Sometimes, while she played Pictures at an Exhibition, Cecilia thought of her father, though the recital was for her mother. She remembered him sitting in his wing chair, one hand supporting his chin, like Rodin's Thinker, his long legs stretched out and his toes flexing in time to a gavotte or a jig. A dance element had crept in as if Anne Elliot or Mary Bennet were seated at the piano and the carpet was being rolled up for an impromptu ball. Her father had not been keen on ritual or commemoration: his strength had been of another kind. Flexible and improvising, he could make the most thought-out suggestion seem casual, as if it had just occurred to him. As she opened Haydn's Sonata in F and pressed down the right-hand corner with her thumb—it was already turned down, meaning her gesture was unnecessary— hot tears stung her eyes for a second. In honour of her father she would not wipe them away.

'Do a thing twice and it becomes a habit,' Zuzanna would say. Warm-hearted, open-armed as she was, she observed her daughters like a hawk. Bottling fruit, sitting at the sewing machine turning yard after yard of material into dresses and shorts and shirts, she missed nothing. Even when other children came to stay—a mother rushed to hospital in the middle of the night, a neighbouring farmer injured in a tractor accident and needing his wife—her welcoming figure was always there at the top of the steps leading to the front door, steps that curved and formed the pattern of a scallop shell.

'I wish she could say no,' Magdalena said to Katharine when their Christmas swelled at the last minute to include sickly-looking twins and a child with a neck brace and an arm in plaster. Still, their resentment evaporated once their mother had drawn a dove on the cast and invited them to join in.

'She was controlling,' Katharine said after one of the recitals, in the pause between drinking several cups of sweet tea and beginning the washing up. For the first time she and Cecilia had come unstuck in the duet. It was only Jesu, Joy of Man's Desiring, a piece so simple they could have played it in their sleep. But somehow they had become entangled and Magdalena had been unable to stop laughing. They had apologised profusely as if their mother really was listening.

William's death had come swiftly. Within twelve hours he had had the first presentiment that this chest pain could not be shrugged off. The ambulance ride with Cecilia beside him—Zuzanna was at a Catholic Women's League meeting and Cecilia had squeezed through the ambulance doors, elbowing aside the St John's attendant, her fierce face the last thing he saw clearly. He gave her a lopsided smile in return, like a crocodile that was eating something, and finally the hospital trolley and the blinding lights of the operating theatre.

Cecilia wandered the corridors while she waited for her mother and sisters to arrive. She tried to eject a cake of chocolate from a slot machine; she drank some water from a paper cup. The windows in the ward were too high for her to see through and she didn't know how to approach a nurse. Occasionally a green-clad surgeon came past. Her mother and sisters bustled in. Clearly her mother was angry with her for sitting beside her father in the ambulance. 'Did he say anything?' she demanded, but Cecilia shook her head. Her mother had no qualms about stopping a surgeon, and soon green-clad bodies were all around her. They talked in lowered voices and Cecilia could not catch a word.

When the funeral was over, Magdalena's store of memories was opened. They came out like ribbons released from a box. The back of the hearse was open and she had stood between Cecilia and Katharine and placed the head of a carnation on the coffin lid. She knew it would fall off when the hearse started up. Someone had dipped the carnation stems in different dyes so they were an unearthly blue, purple or pink. They had not thought of giving him a concert and in any case what could they have played? Katharine was just starting Grade One; no examiner would fall asleep knowing he was in safe hands. Her chubby fingers found it hard to alight in the middle of the keys and sometimes they slid off the black keys as if she were tobogganing down a hill. Cecilia had given up the piano for a term and taken up the violin; Magdalena herself was enrolled for boarding school. 'I hope you'll never go to boarding school,' William said to Cecilia. 'I need someone to go to the movies with me.' She had given him her fervent promise. Dutifully he had sat through The Sound of Music and Mary Poppins and she had watched High Noon and The Man Who Shot Liberty Valance. Their mother, who disliked movies, spent the time in the garden.

As year followed year the three sisters, unless the weather was inclement, went for a walk after the recital in the garden of whichever house it was held in. The rotation was unvaried, apart from one year in which Katharine and Jeremy were building an extension and their piano stayed firmly closed. But whichever garden it was, they were bound to find traces of their mother. A transplanted shrub, an old-fashioned, ferociously thorned rose, a gnarly wisteria. Each had taken something from the herbaceous borders or dug up tiny pansies or bluebells. Their mother's favourite rhododendron, 'Tally Ho', had had a shaky start in Magdalena's garden. It had taken, reluctantly, in the centre of a sloping bed, next to a clump of acanthus. Its trunk was woody, like an old fencepost. The three sisters rounded a bend in the lawn and were staggered to see a blaze of red.

'It's too early, isn't it?' Katharine said. None of the other rhododendrons showed the faintest trace of a bud. 'A message,' Magdalena said. 'After all these years she's saying she approves our recitals.'

But Cecilia, who had gone on ahead, thought it was something in the soil. Perhaps a decomposing stray cat had become their mother's agent? She was such an organiser. And now she had broken through to touch her daughters. The unmistakable red flowers of 'Tally Ho' blazed and blazed.

The Voice

A distant cry stopped me as I followed,
in the island's afternoon heat, the goat track
twisting between the thorn bushes and rocks
around the cliffs above the glittering bay.

Below me, a lone fisherman was singing,
a high, harsh song, careless yet impassioned,
that he kept up even while he heaved the bow
of his turquoise-painted boat against the swell.

I stood there listening, envious and chastened,
as though this were the sound I had longed to hear
through tide on tide of silence and self-doubt,
the voice of one attuned to himself, to life.

A Writer Wrongs

A hater hates
while a waiter waits.
A writer's wry
when the white-out's dry.

While you wander about MOMA or Noma
a little girl has to take a diploma.
(Modern wait staff are a perversity;
they need a paper at a technical university.)

A tomato, to mates,
is a passata as paste.
A potato mutates.
Two tostadas, to taste!

My waiter's waste.
My hater's haste.
So he's a little slapdash down
with a little flat hash brown.

So my fish is pallid.
So there's a little pebble in my freekeh salad.
Is it necessary a balladeer batters
out a ballad?

While I try to wangle my way into a comped meal
and fail, a waiter's patience frays.
While the squealers reel and the reelers squeal
a waiter weighs.

A writer longs
and a long wait angers.
A hater hates
and a writer panders.

A heater heats
a Rita Angus, seen
through the steam from the langoustine
with mangosteen.

And the wait's reprieve:
a writer's right
if a page is white
as a waiter's sleeve.

Home

A swan like a carved radish kickstarts its way across the water.
It should be easier
to temper my words and make iron gates of them,
to remember the names picked out in gold
that echo a memorial garden. I have been
a long way across different water, and Windermere
seems no more surreal
than the flax and puppet shows and long paths I walked on without breathing.
There are nine swans, give or take a miscounting, like a fairytale ration;
two in the Japanese-light balance of the painting in Glasgow. The river
at home is still my Leith, I can still stand
on that spot equally spaced between one rush of water and another,
tune one in, one out, listen to both
while the swan kicks itself around in a spin, leaves its traces
like a white chrysanthemum on the shore I escaped from.

The False Way to the Real

That leaf, its green,
seen by an eye
on turning earth,
lacks constancy.
At night it's blue.

Remove the leaf indoors.
Under the controlled artifice
of a consistent lamp
observe its true, unchanging green—
yet, plucked from its live tree, it browns.

When it comes time to kill the lamp
the leaf will turn into a shade.

REBECCA HAWKES

Cold Speculum

I anchor my eyes away from him, mooring myself in the blue
of a rubber glove balled deep in the rubbish bin. Knees open,

all anticipation, but still shocked by the chill of prising.
Newly aware of all the acts of care I never notice

until they're missing: prongs warmed in a latex-clad hand
or a light brush of inner thigh in vectored warning,

the way one would rest a courteous hand on a mare's rump
so as not to startle when manoeuvring behind her.

Does he think I won't kick? Is it because he's Catholic or something?
Trying not to gentle me as though any implication of tenderness

could make this barely lubricated glowstick somehow sexy?
Even though it's so far from those short weeks ago with you

when we smelled the rain before we could see it, and
heady petrichor rose while a distant cloud unspooled

its load over the alpine fault. That rough tectonic fuck
plates grinding up and down the islands, all upthrust and subduction,

and us unregistered by the Richter scale, quaking
our campground while the sea sucked off the rocks

and the sky bloomed just like the suckled bruise
on a neck, or all my credible fears, blossoming

under my belly to cast roots there, bulbous
as pickling onions, marinating a promise

neither intended to keep. Hence this more perfunctory affair.
You: god-knows-where. Me: gritting my teeth to dilation

under a roof gridded with tiles that look like an upturned swimming pool.
I wish we could do this outside. I would rather look up at the sky

and its well-aerated blue so contrary to drowning, although
I would still be holding my breath

wishing I could get engulfed in something
rather than doing all the damn engulfing.

Add Penetrant to Preferred Broadleaf Herbicide & Devastate the Wildflowers

an overabundance of lupins scours the Mackenzie Country
scorched pestilent   amid shallow rabbit digs & wilding pines
glacial sediment pigmenting lakes
blue as the cyanide-spiked bliss balls we cull wallabies with
Ferafeed 217: Peanut Butter Classic

local farmers are obligated to eliminate the lupins
although a few plant them on purpose   contentiously
providing forage fodder for merino sheep in the high country
they're pretty   these weeds
deep rooted & pernicious   shedding
protein-rich seeds & a kind of shade
that only other unwanteds can live beneath

//
in a carpark on the shore of Lake Tekapo
the rabbit gets shot over and over again
yet will not die

amateur photographers lined up like a firing squad
        as the rabbit hustles into the lupin thicket

        where I crouch low unspotted by the throng
                their lanyards & itineraries
        to snap up unpopulated scenery
        in a picture I will not send you
snow-capped peaks etcetera   & of course the noxious pastel tapestry
                a cheap pixelated sunset
                an aestheticised bruise
plus a flounce of vermin quickness

nibbling oblivious
the rabbit poses for me like warm taxidermy
    half the sun cupped in its silky earlobe
blood vessels ignited petal pink

I expect the photo could win an award at the A&P show
if they hadn't banned pictures of the bloody lupins   the lazy ease
                    of such inconsiderate loveliness

the tour bus moves on   the rabbit and I remain

//

                    all humanity's accomplishments
                    are due to a six-inch layer of topsoil
                    & the fact that it rains

//

        where it won't rain we irrigate
                    until the green believes us
crop circles patrolled by centre pivots
unparching the lucerne   the clover   hieracium
                    this false precipitation this sunshower of effluent
rainbows glinting from the fine spray of shit

//

so much depends on
        whether the sheep are hungry enough
                    to tolerate the taste of toxic alkaloids

as the lupins bloom out the summer in their splendid blushing colonies
both the planters of lupins & their weedkiller neighbours insist
that nature should take its course
                    but they can't agree on what nature means:
conserving shrivelled unpalatable tussock or letting slip
the lupine war on the landscape   floral battalions   a neon-brite rave

        pulsing their heads on the sunset
        a festival of hippies or an invading army
whose thorns do you prefer
sweet briar rosehip or matagouri?

//
the lupins lend their purpleness to prose & I am ill-equipped to be alone
with this sentimental glut
     these unearned emotions   this too-easy picturesque
     florid & fecund & phallic   all guzzle & loll
     choking the riverbed with sex
ovaries & stamens   orbicular pods   naked waxen stems
little pink hoods yielding   like skin inside out
where I become the ghost of an orchid
fallow on linens which still reek   of cross-pollination
        I suppose you could say
I haven't buried the hatchet   I am still swinging it
in my splintered fist   I am building a tiny house with it
in the Mackenzie Country
because I cannot live inside you

//
meanwhile the lupins   wring out their bright disaster of seeds
in the riverbed & propagate downstream

The Beekeepers

i.
My father kept bees at the bottom
Of his garden. Once without gear
On he disturbed a hive. The drones
Rose, felt out for him, glanced against his skin.
My father dashed back across the lawn,
Directly towards the baby

In her arms. The baby under the shawl
He'd muttered *over cautious*
All over as she'd rearranged it. She has told me
About having to stand across the lawn
From a man perfectly distracted,
About the moment when

The algorithm was triggered,
The evening walk gave out and his gaze
Latched on to the apiary
As if he held a conical flask
Delicately between thumb and forefinger.
She says she felt his fingers itch

Before he touched the hive lid.
His flight back to her, drawing bees
(only riled enough to see him off)
Towards the soft swollen limbs she had
Veiled, was secondary really, less striking
Than his complete predictability.

ii.
We model a swarm of bees as electrons
In a box, simultaneous equations which
Must be solved through iterative methods.

It is not possible to predict the movements
Of an individual vibrating particle in open
Space. It is not possible to predict

The outcome of a measurement.
Even an electron cloud can be unruly
Even the harmonics of a hive can

Collapse. Open the box and often the
Bee has been unsealed, the sting is
Embedded and the energy released.

iii.
My child mind hatched bees
magnified. They were well defined

in space and time, not the four-legged flies
Aristotle described for centuries.

There used to be a rest stop
on the way to Palmerston. They had

a glass hive in a dark room
to display the comb, golden and

restless, and a Perspex tube to funnel
the bees outside. I could have

watched them longer even though
I loved our mother and the drive

up to the farm. She was the one
who drew my attention to the

waxy hexagons, the yellow dust
clumped on their black hairs.

She bought me a pink plastic
compound eye. She told me about

tomb honey, left for pharaohs, tasted
by archaeologists.

We'd buy bee balls to suck in
the car. They came in mānuka,

clover and brown striped with
venom added. In the homestead I watched

a bee muddle around my arm hair while
I was lying on a sun-soaked cell

of carpet, lazy as a grub. I said Mum
there's something coming out

of its abdomen then oh!
You said they wouldn't sting if I was still.

iv.
Most honey isn't what it used to be.
I grew up amongst mānuka scrub, I know
a bloke from high country who let the land

degrade to bush because the swarms extract more
from minding their own business. Every year
his crop's refined to higher grade.

He implants what he can:
variegation, branching angle, ensuring the
buds ease open to the ideal moment. And it's odd

because these bees are foreign workers,
moving through the trees like enzymes,
strange catalysts for our wild flowers.

v.
I think of Dad the moment after he
Unsealed the hive and reverted by instinct
To my mother. Late spring, a day so cold

He'd wondered how the bees were doing,
Imagined himself an observer who makes
No measurements, has no impact on

Results. Perhaps he thought he could run
The sequence over, reiterate from initial conditions,
Return to our side and start the test again.

Negligence in the absence of malice but now,
Twenty years later, there are afternoons I find I am
In my father's apiary watching his fingers itch.

Plaster Cast

There are people running around on the roof. I hear their footfall over dinner and late into the darkness, they thunder through my sleep.

'Up with you now, Sleepyhead,' my mother calls and I ring slow along the hallway. Beneath the bell of my nightgown my two feet are clappers, made to be dangled.

At the kitchen table is bread and cheese and not a crumb from yesterday's meals. My mother licks her finger and presses the crumbs into her mouth. These days all the mice in the house are wet-nosed fingers.

'It was that lot,' I point a knife to the ceiling, 'running around on the roof.'

'Don't be daft,' my mother says, patting my baby brother's back. 'The roof's too slopey.'

My baby brother is an unfilled kettle. He splutters and starts, not understanding the hollow sound he makes. 'Fill me from the tap!' he cries. 'Heat me! Heat me! Heat me!'

I step outside to find crocodiles patrolling the street. They snap this way and that. Eye of pocket watch, claw of denture, tails made of tangled human hair.

I fling to the neighbours, clanging, but the neighbours are ghosts. They hover a foot off the ground though they're wanting to touch it. Pull me down, their eyes say.

'Can you see from up there, who's running around on our roof?' I ask, but they only look at me with empty mouths and point inside their own hearts.

'Can you hear them, though? They run through the night.' But the ghosts only turn their backs to me and cradle their ribs.

But there *are* people running around on the roof. Their footfall sends trails of plaster dust into my hair until my mother has to say, 'Don't be daft, it's only dandruff.'

Privet

At thirteen I developed
asthma, out of the blue. My desperate
parents searched for the culprit. Was it the ivy
flowering its limey bullets along the wall?
Or the privet, staring starrily
out of its young green brain? A leaflipped
Catholic girl skipping to confirmation
with a corsage spray and white trashpearls.
I liked to look at it flowering this way
while I sat outside to avoid
the raised hairtrigger voices
that switched on one bright morning and never stopped.
But in the end a verdict was reached
and the privet had to go.

Friendly Fire

Joan de Lestonnac was born almost 500 years ago.
As usual, it was her friends who betrayed her
in the end, making sure she was treated with contempt
every day in the establishment she had set up.
Nothing hurts like the arrow from a friend's bow.
Like being blindsided by a kiss
in a dark, derelict garden.
For the record I saw you there
with your hoodie pulled up
over your head. Full of such ordinary poison.
I think you saw me too through the thin veneer
of the rain. All you could do was finger a coin,
its heavy gold some cold
comfort, turning over and over again.

Betty as a Boy

Your New Zealand mother and American stepfather wanted boys,
and that is why, you think, you and your closest sister, the one you are
not related to at all, dressed like Annie Hall. The patterned tie,
textured tweed, taupe-hued tailoring over mannish knitwear,
waistcoat and tie.

You and she together, the endlessness of the Oldsmobile, the long
blue motels of the Southwest, sharing beds that creaked with the gravity
of a thousand whispering bodies, building a family between the two of you
while only metres away in the double bed, your mother was
just another young woman, joining herself to anger.

You were never the favourite, you were the sad one from the old life,
the needy one who crawled into the shower with your mother, longing
so hard to be loved that she couldn't take it any more, and punched you,
nine years old, square in your soft, desperate face.

Now your sister, the one you're not related to at all, lives in the hills of
California, in an austere house surrounded by thirsty cacti—prickly pear,
parodia, barbary fig, saguaro—with her ex-jock husband,
and you in the Far North of New Zealand,
on a rocky outcrop over the silver Pacific, alone.

Your American and New Zealand lives seem to have calibrated into
expected rhythms, she pressing organic oranges into elixir, you
a salty chardonnay, she yoga and you ocean.

But at night your sister places her neat body down in the long,
cool shadow of the saguaro, and sews together the eyes of a lizard with a
cactus spine and spider's silk as thread. In her waking life, so Californian,
tanned and usual, at night, like all of us—fragmented and orbiting herself
like a stranger.

She's read too much Carlos Castaneda, smuggled too many boatloads of
drugs from Colombia to Santa Cruz, taken too much peyote to be your
average dream-girl with a rearranged nose. She knows cacti like a
cheerleader knows the lonely hours waiting on the inside of a letter jacket.
But she knows that too.

And you, outside the upmarket grocer's, camouflaged top, khaki pants
slashed with a silk of red, a backpack strung with things that clink,
disappearing into your androgyny—the inverse of a newly minted drag queen,
appearing like a flaming comet, burning to be noticed.

SUSAN WARDELLL

Grain of her Voice

They say
when meaning is gone, all that is left
is the grain
of the voice.

Well, hers sweeps the room like salt-flecked taffeta.
She says
it rained the night of the St Clair dance,
and though time has carved
sudden cliffs in the story,
she remakes the dress each day
with words that fall like wheat threshed in shadow,
till fear pulls at its pin-tucked form,
places a seamless and immodest silence
in its place.

They often find her undressed
in just the skin of her sound,
petticoats wet with the rivulets
that run down her sentences
like sand,
slip underground.

The grumbling hymn of the road unknown,
the tussock-whispers of slippers
seeking terra firma,
The rough boot-print of *home*,
The hiss of the sea hot against
the vinyl grind before the first strain of symphony—

Dust in its veins—
And the low moon-stretched croon, love-hush,
of nervous fingers rubbing at oiled silk.

Yes it poured down, pours down,
sound leaks through
as she keens, a gull call,
a thrush in the field—or was she elsewhere,
with him, not you?

The sea roars, laughs itself horse-racing-back-to-shore,
only not so sure,
for when she wandered
they used to offer her warm milk,
but they don't any more: too pale.

When she grinds teeth in her sleep,
and lips crack like
speakers crackle, creak, and speak,
smooth back the sheets,
the hair, loose on her forehead
and let the sound pour out.

The sound
pours out.

When I let my mind's grip
on the semantics of noise
slip
I can still sense the shape of her
through the rain, I can hear it
in her voice—
in its grain.

Feral

The kids at the end of the camp were young and rowdy. They had no furniture, shower bags or even towels by the look of it. They got their food daily from the service station, but had brought plenty of booze—beers for the boys and alcopops for the girls. At night they brought out the spirits. There were four or five guys and three girls—they seemed to come and go a bit—and they were all in their prime.

They slept until at least midday and stayed up into the early hours of the morning, their rhythm enviably leisurely, and sauntered around the site with their young bodies relaxed and oily.

The girls kept together throughout the afternoon, moving slowly; conspiratorially in pairs, or in a cluster in the sun. They were on their phones, played cards and flicked through magazines, tapping away to their individual tunes.

The guys stuck together during the day too. They took longer to get going but when the sun was at its hottest, in the early afternoon, they became wildly active, throwing and kicking balls and wrestling while they got the rods and boards sorted. They shouted and laughed and strutted to fill as much of the bleached space as possible. They marked and remarked their territory and the girls they had brought with them.

When they came back to the camp from fishing and surfing they would light a fire and play rough ball games. The girls would rise on their forearms, tilt their heads up to watch them from under their damp floppy brims. They couldn't keep their eyes off the marauding boys, as if they themselves could never move like that, weighted by the day of doing nothing, heavy and hot with sun.

They lacked the boys' enviable physicality; the easy way in which they occupied and commanded their bodies. As if the girls were trapped on the floor of an ocean through which their teeming boys caroused. These young men: they flung themselves around, no idea how beautiful they were, here, in their prime, their bodies lean and strong while the soft sunken parts at the back of their long necks kept something of their boyhoods, the memory of their mothers' nuzzle.

There was something soft and childish about the girls too. Flashes of it remained. You saw it in the curl of their bodies sleeping off a hangover, and later again, when they stretched into animation, in that beautiful unself-conscious reach before wakefulness. You saw it in the dorky way they held out their plastic plates to the boys for their burnt sausage or bit of fish, unsure how to take their jokes, or whether they were being invited into the ribbing. And you saw it in their pleasure, their sometimes shy but pleased faces.

They were so happy! Ruth stared at them ravenously. She coveted their leisurely teenage limbs, their slow animal unfolding at dusk and their full awakening at night. She stared at their bodies and the way the girls lay, tumbled together in a warm slovenly mess. The way they were so tempting, these young girls, as well as confounding, to the boys circling them. They were gorgeous, these girls, even when they weren't especially; gorgeous because they were young and occupied their leisure in the way of a sated animal. They had nothing yet to lose, and they were perfect in their neat pack of three. The perfect number, Ruth remembered: a triptych. Two could be dangerous because if one went down, willingly or not, the other was stranded. Three freed one up to get it together with someone or lose it without letting the side down.

Ruth was pretty certain she knew which one was angling for action. Over the course of the long weekend she watched this one especially. This one so different from herself but the sort of girl she had often been friends with. 'I'm frightened by the devil / And I'm drawn to those that ain't afraid,' sang Joni Mitchell knowingly in 'A Case of You'.

This one, the smallest and darkest, would get it together with at least two of the guys, Ruth wagered. She was outrageous even while seemingly asleep. Everything was designed for the boys' pleasure. She kept her nipples erect (how did she do that?) and whenever the boys came close she bristled. She had great tits, this little one, and she used them, wearing coarse see-through linen tops and keeping her buttons unbuttoned. The boys were helpless before her. She was so small and busty and with a great red mouth. The other girls looked like mild fawns next to this one. Or dopey calves.

86

She was a pushy little thing, switching her tail and pushing her hard pointy head. She was the quivering intense little cat that leaves a trace of saliva when pushing her head in your palm. She couldn't get enough of pressure. The other girls were prettier, but nowhere near as sexy. They had no idea, the other two (which has its own charms). Altogether, Ruth could see, the three girls were a killer combination. Those girls could hitchhike from Auckland to Wellington in under nine hours.

'Stop staring, Mum!' the kids demanded. 'Why are you so obsessed with them?'

'I'm just imagining what they're like,' Ruth explained. 'I'm just people-watching. It's anthropological. It's material for my book.'

But really she was imagining herself with them. Slowly waking, hungover and horny. Eating only when you feel like it and only enough to get to the next phase. Inhabiting your body the way sand fills a sack. Loving your friends amorphously, with all your soft heart. Feeling drenched in the friendship, the closeness of your friends. Maybe feeling the hardness of one of the boys' bodies at some point in the night. Definitely swimming naked, in phosphorescence. Diving into dark water and for a moment having absolutely no idea which way is up to the surface and loving that moment, lost and disoriented in the total cold darkness suddenly illuminated by the shining bubbles outlining another body diving in or your own foot kicking, your hands waving in front of your blissfully drunken face.

'Just stop staring; it's embarrassing.'

In her own camp things were good too. There were cards and swimming and the deeply satisfying sight of seeing your own child asleep under a pōhutukawa tree wrapped in the torn lavalava that used to hang over a window in your flat.

This is happiness, Ruth thought, this is life. And she believed it.

Taking your bowl of beans to the moss-covered wooden gate and leaning against it, with your face smiling into the setting sun. Your husband making the children laugh. Eating your dinner while marvelling at how strong and perfectly constructed spiders' webs are, and pointing at wood pigeons noisily flopping around, at tūī rushing around in a fever, at fat bees lazily taking a late tour of the even fatter lavender. The hot yellow field and the high old blue sky with the shape of the pūriri tree against it. This too is happiness, Ruth knew.

87

'I don't want a hairy fanny,' Mary announced as she looked newly critically at her mother's body. Ruth was naked, on her knees, awkwardly bent forward looking for something in the tent. She was conscious of the fact that Mary's was not the most flattering view. The backs of her thighs, when positioned like this, came up in large hand-widths of dimples, and her small breasts hung emptily down like sad little mice. Even the tops of Ruth's arms wobbled these days, and her tummy, while still slim, was dry and saggy. The skin all over was marked and drying out and rough to touch.

'Well, you'll have a hairy fanny one day, you know,' Ruth responded, 'to keep the bugs out.'

That sounded ridiculous and Mary cringed at the idea. She wanted her mother to be beautiful at all times. But she also wanted her mother not to stand out. It was confusing. Right now she wished her mother's body was evenly tanned and smooth. She wished Mummy had long, clean hair that came straight down and she wished that her mother wore shoes with spikes on them when she came—as she did rarely—to pick her up from school. And she really didn't like it when Ruth sang as she walked, she decided now as her mother hummed a silly made-up tune.

My God, Ruth thought, she's only seven and it's started already. She sat back on her haunches and felt briefly ashamed, even apologetic. She could see the flashes of disappointment, of impatience, in her daughter's eyes.

'Just hurry up and get dressed, Mum,' Mary commanded as she turned and walked out of the tent. Her young body had strengthened and grown so much since last summer, the protruding belly flattening out to give a new shape, the shape of a girl. *Thou art thy mother's glass, and she in thee | Calls back the lovely April of her prime*—Ruth remembered the lines. She wasn't quite ready to acquiesce and felt a shiver in her lower back.

'Look at your mother—she's a mermaid,' Ruth had heard Ryan say to the children when she emerged from the sea that morning. It was what he always said when she came out of the water but the children were no longer convinced. Last summer Mary had still sort of believed it, but this summer she was clearly irritated by her mother and her mother's body. There were too many things in the wrong place. The hair and the lumps and the bumps needed reorganising, Mary thought, so in the sand she drew pictures of mermaids with seaweed for hair over and over again, and then, frowning, took a stick and scratched them out.

Ruth loved peeing in the long grass and shaking herself dry. She loved the dark shift in the sand and the warm salty stench when she squatted down. She even loved the possibility that the pee would catch her ankle or pool at her feet. At night it was even better. In the real night, when even the teenagers were sleeping and the sky lit knowingly and expansively, as if it had opened up for the important business of the day, Ruth liked to pee on the beach with the stars pinging above her. The sea was so much louder then, too, insisting on its arrival, demanding to be let in, like a cat crashing through its flap in the early morning. She loved the quick run on her toes back to the tent and unzipping the tent and crawling on her hands and knees, with wet sticky feet, into the warmth of her man, to spoon—the tree brushing against the damp sagging roof of the tent, the waves sorting out the sand and the children close enough to touch.

On the last night of their camp, Ruth felt about as happy as she'd ever been. She always got to this place on their holidays. There she sat, under their pōhutukawa tree, with a glass of wine, watching the kids run wild. By the end of the holiday they were mostly naked and dirty. Nice and feral, Ruth thought, the way children should be.

Across the way, the girls were up and getting dressed in short denim shorts, tight fluorescent singlets and loose cotton shirts. The boys had come in off the water and the rocks with their sunburns and their swagger. Two of them had caught fish and knew how to prepare and cook it. Someone had gone and got packs of Sizzlers and some ice. They moved into a circle around their fire, cooking and talking and drinking and then, quite suddenly but very keenly, Ruth yearned to be with them, with their sense of come what may, with their sense of the boundlessness of the night and their existence in it. Ruth knew the exact shape of things to come for her. That was the thing about having a family; it was a set pattern and sometimes you just had to blur those lines a little to recapture a glimpse of the great expanse beyond.

Her kids had been over there a few times since last night, when Thomas had been invited to join in a game of football with the boys. Mary had gone over too, and sat with the girls, no doubt talking about Taylor Swift. They had painted her toenails the new orange and put one of their porkpie hats on her head. Ruth had watched from a distance, wishing she could join in, envying her daughter her easy camaraderie. Then she'd reprimanded herself, told herself off for wanting to be like her children, like a tragic yummy mummy who from behind might look like a teenager but is an old woman really, too old certainly to be getting around in white jeans and drinking in bars with her teenage daughters the way she'd heard some of the mothers at school did.

They needed something now—Ruth could tell with her mother's intuition. She hoped they would come and ask her, as they had on the first night. They had needed a pot for noodles, which they'd kept all weekend. Tonight they wanted sauce, one of the boys called out from a distance. He was walking towards her but had finished talking by halfway across. He was so casual, so comfortable in his sense of entitlement that he would get what he needed from the lady with the kids, that Ruth felt flattered, as if she had been handpicked. She felt absurdly pleased to have an excuse to go over, so that she decided to take her glass of wine too. She might have a little chat with them, she thought as she walked across the campground, pleased she had not put on her old yoga pants after all and was still wearing her cute sundress and wide-brimmed hat held on with salty scarf.

Thomas and Mary were there too and rolled their eyes at their mother, making it clear they didn't want her muscling in on what they had with the older kids. Ruth stood by the barbecue and chatted in her friendliest teacher voice. These were good kids, she thought to herself. She liked kids with spunk but also with manners. Kids who had been brought up to look adults in the eye and hold a conversation with them. Yes, they'd had a good weekend, no they hadn't been here before, yes the fishing was good—would you like a bit of fish? We've got heaps ... The chat petered out and Ruth felt superfluous, so she waved an awkward goodbye and wandered back to her camp with her empty glass and her bit of schnapper in her hand.

'I'll see my two soon, to get ready for bed!' she called back over her shoulder.

After the kids had crawled into their tent, Ruth poured herself the rest of the wine and kept watching the camp down the other end. They had moved together closer and grew louder as the sky darkened and the stars turned on. She wanted to go back to join them—maybe she could go over and thank them again for the fish, which Ryan had cooked with rosemary on the grill, and they had eaten with their hands. But she lost her nerve. They had turned into themselves now, gorgeously self-obsessed, self-contained. They had got what they needed from the others on the site and did not need to give them another thought.

But when they set off to the beach, Ruth could not help but follow them.

From the short distance she took up her watch of the dark one. She knew that one; the way she kept herself ready, and enjoyed imagining the ease with which she invited the boys to partake. The tide murmured over the sand, licking its lips, smacking itself on the body of the land. The sea—it was always there; it had to be, thought Ruth. That's why she could never have lived in London or Berlin or New York. She could not imagine it, inland and stranded, for any length of time; or so she told herself.

She had brought down their last bottle of wine and sat on the cold sand and drank straight from the bottle. Ryan would have seen where she was headed and stayed behind.

She would always love that feeling of expansion that comes with alcohol coursing through. She stared up to the sky, straining, wanting something, unsure what, listening to the crowd from the tent along at the end of the beach. They were drunk too, but loud and confidently so. She wanted to form profound thoughts, the beginnings of stories and poems in her mind, but she was too distractedly drawn to the sound of the group. You could not clearly make out what they were saying, but they whooped and laughed and jostled. They got up and started moving along the foreshore towards where Ruth lounged a little way back from the water on a dune.

They moved in a messy formation, front lit by the reflection from the white foamy water, like a scene in a music video. So pleased with themselves, and why wouldn't they be? Some had arms around one another, some were pushing and pulling. They carried their drinks and blankets and wood, like Bacchus and his train of revellers under a cobalt blue-black sky. Ruth did not want them to see her so she pressed herself flat against the dunes as they passed closely by before settling down about four or five metres in front of her, between Ruth and the water.

'Hey Lauren, come swimming,' she heard the guy who had gutted the fish call. Lauren was the little dark one, but she was folded into someone else tonight. Ruth had watched her slim legs trip-trapping between the bigger

calves as they caroused down the beach towards her. Lauren was *an easy lay*—
Ruth formed the juvenile phrase in her head, enjoying the mean twang. And
this was the perfect night for it—who would let her go? It was one of the
other two who replied, 'I'll come.' This girl had trailed a little, was relatively
quiet. She was the one who had carefully painted Mary's toenails and sung
Taylor Swift songs with her, the one Mary had swooned over when she was
back in her tent, writing in her journal.

'I will,' she said again, to no one in particular. Not in a sad way, but quietly
determined. She had already stood up and she was drunk too; Ruth could tell
from the awkward way she stood, legs apart, and twisted to get her shirt over
her head. She giggled and wriggled and Ruth fought a strong motherly urge
to help the silly child get her top off without ripping the delicate fabric. But
she managed and Ruth stayed put and the girl's body beneath the clothes was
surprisingly lovely, lit blue in the thin light.

She was unassuming and strong and lean. She had a plain pink bikini
bottom on, no top and a good even tan. She was like a fit young boy, really,
and as soon as she was ready she turned and ran, her body and arms reaching
out towards the sea and straight into it. She didn't wait for anyone, and the
boy who had called for a swim made no move to join her.

Ruth stood up, feeling the full effect of the wine now, and stripped off her
jeans and T-shirt. She had talked herself into it, into the idea that this was her
night too. She removed her bra and her undies, carried away with the idea of
the evening and her role in it, and ran towards the water. When she passed
the group on the beach she heard their jangled surprise, even gasps. They
really hadn't noticed her in the dunes and recoiled a little, as if they had been
splashed, when she came near. One of them wolf-whistled, before they all
laughed in a mix of ridicule and embarrassment.

Naked under the moon, Ruth had to be tenacious; to get away with this she
had to be confident, believe fully in her glorification of the night. She forced
her face to fix upwards in an open-mouthed smile and kept running. All the
while aware of the wobbling flesh on her big bottom and her skinny jiggling
boobs, she cantered into the water, her legs splaying a little at the shock of
the cold water, thinking about pubic hair—no doubt shocking to this bald
generation—and her ugliness as she faced the girl arching out of an
incoming wave.

The girl in the water briefly struggled to balance, to take in the unexpected woman in front of her who was waving and smiling.

'Hi! Isn't it beautiful?', Ruth called as if they knew each other; as if they were old friends. The girl's face took a moment to register who the older woman was, then shifted quickly from brief, shocked, recognition to hostility. The anger was so incongruous in the small passive face, the quiet eyes. She changed utterly, devastatingly. As she struggled through the foam and tripped past Ruth, she didn't take her eyes off the older woman, as if to keep her at bay. She looked furious, resentful, and then Ruth heard again the mocking laughter as the girl rejoined her friends, who surrounded her and took her back up the beach.

When they moved off in a huddle to their camp their laughter turned down a few notches to a low rumble, broken by the odd wolf-whistle and peal of laughter ricocheting across the beach while Ruth swam, both mortified and exhilarated, in the night sea.

ERIK KENNEDY

Today

The rabbit does not hop in her brisk way.
The artist can't imagine anything.
The hill declines the tenderness of fogs.
The soap diminishes in many hands.
The car refuses once again to start.
The isotope continues to decay.
The chair awaits the sitter, who is late.
The building segregates its occupants.
The cliff resigns an outcrop to the sea.
The window jams and won't let in the breeze.
The mould spores screw their way into the bread.
The tree ignores its greeny symmetry.
The dog laments her owner in the yard.
And I, alone and glad, have missed these things.

Tick Boxes

☐ to receive news of the clinic's special offers
☐ to say you would like a copy of our letter to your doctor
☐ to indicate current conditions and medications
☐ to express a wish that your next of kin be notified should you suffer a medical emergency during detoxification

Now, tick all boxes that apply to you and your situation:

☐ I drink alone
☐ I am prone to violence when I drink
☐ Alcohol is the first thing I think of when I get up
☐ I don't get out or socialise much
☐ I hide or hoard alcohol in my house
☐ I rely on drink to improve my mood
☐ I have only a small appetite—food does not interest me
☐ I have proven vitamin deficiencies
☐ I make little effort with my grooming
☐ My home is not as clean as it used to be
☐ When I have not had a drink for some time, I shake/become mean or unreasonable

If there were a pill you could take that would make you sick as soon as a sip of liquor touched your lips, would you take it?

Yes ☐   No ☐

We thought so.

KATHRYN MADILL

A Catalogue of Belonging

1. *Over Wide Green Seas*, 2018, monoprint, 200 x 295 mm.
2. *A Common Tale (1)*, 2018, monoprint, 70 x 90 mm.
3. *The Chorus (2)*, 2018, monoprint, 60 x 180 mm.
4. *The Night House*, 2018, monoprint, 60 x 180 mm.
5. *The Chorus (3)*, 2017, monoprint, 240 x 850 mm.
6. *The Chorus (4)*, 2017, monoprint, 240 x 850 mm.
7. *The House Party*, 2018, monoprint, 320 x 430 mm.
8. *The Chorus (5)*, 2017, monoprint, 200 x 295 mm.

All images courtesy of the artist; photography by Justin Spiers; IT assistance Victoria McIntosh

I have found this life of making art is like a life of learning another language, a new vocabulary made up of images accumulated over the years.

Within this new series of monoprints, figures move through imagined rooms and landscapes in search of their own sense of place.

The monoprinting process allows me to combine the qualities of both paint and print, the immediacy of the drawn line when wiping back the ink, and always the anticipation of what will be revealed once the plate has travelled through the press.

—Kathryn Madill

The People Between the Silences

If I tell her this one last thing about me, I'll probably lose her. But I probably will anyway if I say nothing, so I can't keep quiet any more.

I know Min is it, because I've been around long enough to recognise when people are good for each other. And she has too. We don't say it out loud, but we both know that this is the one we don't mess up. She mustn't see me as too damaged or weird for her because she doesn't need any more of that. When she sees that she walks.

It's been good. Almost three years and we are steady, practical people now. There's the business. We get up in the morning when we know we should, and we get on and do the things we need to do until they are done. We do life properly—for ourselves, and even more for each other. Because we've tried the other way and it didn't work.

I've been famous most of my life for fucking up perfectly good things that looked impossible to derail. And she's been far too good at putting up with men like me who all did that. But we met clean, Min and I, stepping out of our own trails of wreckage. We found each other that day, and told the truth. We made a little window of light.

'Honesty—it's at the heart of you and me,' she always says, and she's right. But I hug her quickly at that moment so she can't see my eyes.

I haven't killed anyone. I've done nothing dramatic or illegal. I just see things; I see people. People who shouldn't be there. Not all the time, or every day. I can't explain because I don't understand it myself. But she would assume it was a hangover from the drugs and booze. She grew up with that shit all around and she's had enough for one lifetime, and fair enough.

So if I told her I saw things sometimes that other people didn't, she wouldn't attack me or anything, or invite the drug squad in to turn the place over. But she would walk away. Because she's learned to do that, and look at her now—you can see she's right. She's strong and doing it right. Because she's learned to leave instead of maiming herself trying to save all the broken people around her.

So anyway, what happens is that I will see someone, just out, like anyone else. But there will be something about them that doesn't look right. Often it's their clothes I notice first. On a day warm enough for just a T-shirt, they might have on a jumper and jacket too—but not look bothered by being so overdressed. Or I might pass them out walking on a muddy track, but in clean shoes. Then they disappear.

When I got to 19 or 20 and finally accepted what was going on, I got brave and started speaking to them. Mostly about the place, about the day, the weather. They can't generally talk about anything else, and it bothers them if I ask. They turn away. It's called audiovoyance or something when you can hear and speak to them as well as see them. I think that's it, but I don't look into it or ask around.

I don't think it's from a smack on the head—falling over pub steps or coming off the bike or getting coathangered. Because I saw these people before that, when I was a kid. I just didn't admit it back then.

I've told a couple of mates but only when I knew they were pissed enough not to remember in the morning. Because it's not the sort of thing I wanted people talking about, about me. Especially not to Min.

When she was about 14 or 15, maybe even younger, she had this boy she really liked. He was pretty sensible I think, doing better than most at school—like her, and I can imagine the two of them planning how they would get out and do everything differently. He had an elder brother who always had drugs, but this lad, the one she was with, he kept away.

One night though, when he was watching the footy upstairs with his brother and a few older mates, just for a laugh they stuck a tab of acid in his drink when he was fetching more chips.

Their mother came home later and looked up and saw him stood there balancing on the balustrading over the stairwell talking to himself. She couldn't get there in time to stop him diving like he was bungy jumping or hang gliding or something. He only fell one floor but there was lots to hit on the way down.

They cleared him from hospital after a few weeks, saying there was nothing wrong now—he was all fixed. But he wasn't. Apparently he wasn't the same bloke any more. Either the head injury or the LSD had changed some wiring. And Min didn't like the new one, the lying bastard they sent home. Few people did.

She had too many around her like that, over the years. Different drugs, but similar stories and the same endings. And then there were the usual social drinkers with too many friends. Like I used to be. Bright enough to find reasons to do the wrong things day after day, until all the good things have gone, including the memory.

Min was like her mother—a carer. She cared for everybody, but there were too many of them. Finally, the twat from Geelong did a runner with just about everything she had. That Christmas she went for a lie-down at her mum's after lunch and didn't get up again properly until they were writing the cards for the next one. The doctors called it various things, but Abby never saw it as medical. She just put her daughter on a 'love drip', as she called it. Kept away the damaged and needy who drained her, and let the girl slowly put enough back in the tank to stand again.

When she rejoined the world it was on different terms. It had to be.

I would talk to our doc if I could guarantee she'd say I was solid. But I don't want to risk the visit leading to bad stuff. Because it's never felt like it's something wrong with me. When I look at Google it says hallucinations can happen when the body is highly stressed, like mountaineers or people running races across the desert. But it doesn't feel like that. When the army and I were still an item, I got so shattered alone on one night exercise that by the early morning I couldn't read the map or see the track to take—even though it was right in front of me. I sat myself down for a few minutes by a lake and drank and ate what I had left. Within minutes everything became obvious and normal again.

But I didn't see anyone who shouldn't have been there, and that deprivation felt completely different. Being tired beyond words shut things down in me, whereas when I see these people I feel like it's because how I see the world has opened further up. That's all I can say really, because like I said I don't understand it. There is a silence around them, but otherwise I am more aware, not less. And I've got used to it.

Mostly it's when I'm on foot, but once I saw someone in a car on the motorway. He appeared alongside me driving a 1990s faded blue Toyota or

Nissan, and stayed there for a few minutes. A young guy, worried about something, looking straight ahead with dark scared eyes. After a while he eased back behind me and I watched him in the mirrors. Then as he went through my blind spot he disappeared. There was no exit nearby and the road was clear behind me for a kilometre or two.

I've seen Min do it—shut off and cut people out when she feels she must. The daughter of an old friend of hers asked to crash on the sofa bed last summer. Just for a couple of nights. When she arrived I went and got a takeaway and this girl—Bel—produced a load of wine, drank most of it, and as the evening went on she started talking about her mate who could tell you your past lives, and how she'd been sceptical but now believed it. She'd been told she could do it too, she had the gift, and said she had already picked things up about us. So she just started coming out with stuff about me and about Min.

I knew Bel's mum had lost a few years to drugs at that age and as we listened to this weird shit getting weirder, both of us wondered about her girl. Her eyes weren't right. And she said things you don't say to people you barely know. I didn't argue or anything, I mean, who am I to say what's real and what isn't? But when Bel got onto how miscarriages—we've had two—were often punishments carried over from previous lives, but that she could take us to meet their souls, Min just got up, went out the back and rang Bel's mum. When she came back in Min just told her to pack and go, and stood watching until she did. It was dark and getting late and I gave her taxi money and a bit extra because I felt bad.

So I know how definite she is now, Min.

Today was different for me. In all the years I've seen these people they have always been strangers. Never someone I knew. But this morning Min's mum died.

At about ten or a bit after, but I didn't know that. Nor did Min straightaway, because she was at ours still doing the GST before going up the Home to see her. And at about that time I was stopped at the lights, looked across and saw Abby, Min's mum, in her favourite coat and hat at her old bus stop in Hataitai waiting to go through the tunnel into town. She had her workbag and was stood enjoying the sun, looking like she did before the fall. I watched her for a few seconds but she didn't look my way, and then the lights changed and by the time I could pull out of the traffic and go back she wasn't there any more.

Instead of going back to the job in Newtown I just headed round, got on the motorway at The Terrace and went slowly towards the Home where she'd been since the op. I didn't know what to do but this felt right. I didn't call Min because there was nothing I could say. I was just waiting and hoping.

I was just before Petone when the phone rang in my jacket in the back of the cab. I let it go to message, because it would have been unusual if I didn't when I was supposed to be working. Min just said the Home had called and could I come straightaway and meet her there. I pulled into Petone and drove down the waterfront to kill time. I sat and watched the ferry heading out and thought about Abby. We'd got on well, me and Min's mum. And I was proud of that, because it was a first for me—having a mother see me as someone who could care for her girl.

As I sat there a friend of Min's came slowly past with her dog. There was nowhere to hide and she'd have known the truck anyway. We spoke for a minute and then I drove off to the Home.

Min saw me arrive just as she was walking in. I had got there too fast from the job at that time of day. She asked why but I offered no excuse because I'm a crap liar. And then I just couldn't look surprised and empty enough when she told me what the nurses had said.

When she and I sat with the body I could tell my reaction was all wrong. I was just too prepared, one or two steps on, but how could she know that.

Min just looked at me, confused for a while and then suspicious and then deeply hurt and I saw something start to switch off behind her eyes. This woman I need utterly was looking at yet another man who had either been pretending to be honest with her all along—or was pretending now. It amounted to the same.

And so right here I need to explain about this last part of me. Because she's going to walk.

Nails

You
My baby is craniofacially flawed.
weigh
My baby is born a wilted orchid.
the
My baby is a mouthful of broken sprockets.
nails
My baby calls himself a prophet.
in
My baby is wrists with red-beaded lines.
your
My baby sticks bliss in his veins.
hands

TONY BEYER

Winter Feed

rolled into neat bundles
behind the moving machine

as if the land itself
aspect and prospect

had been harvested and stored
in memory

       slow-burning suns
rains that delayed

for days this garnering
and tight among the withered thistles

stalks the weight of lovers
might have bruised

or hares' or magpies' footprints
tilted for a second out of true

all sealed by close and stifling shadow
for the longer cold

for dawns the breaths of cattle
cloud with warmth

MICHAEL HALL

Late Summer's Pigs

So hot, they barely raise a grunt, let alone
an oink, even the runt's got big, his belly

rising and falling in the iron truncated shade.
One will get up, like an ignored moon,

at midday and wander over to the trough
to snout the sludge and dried mud. But

today's burning. The bigger one raises his
head at my approach, half expecting slops

or milk, then plonks it down. You get in,
give them both a scratch, the big one first,

along his back, behind his ear, dry skin and
hair, the way they look you in the eye

is human, which makes you human too.
Above the plateau an invisible mass of heated air

is rising; by mid-afternoon, just before milking,
dark clouds will grumble on the ranges, fill

the plain, before great drops will fall, detonate in
the track dust; then it will really open up, on

the raft of cows set drifting from the paddocks
toward the shed. Standing, staring out, those two

in the rain, watch my dad, discipled by our dog,
through the netted and sagging guts of wire.

Drought

After mother died, father said
he'd get used to living alone
the way rye grass gets used
to living without rain.

After weeks, he lost
his vigour but remained
resolute, the way thirsty
karo leaves lose their shine
yet hold onto branches.

Soon, he would slip
at the gate the way brittle
leaves lose their grip.

He fell on the concrete path
and screamed, I can
get up by myself,
like a blown-down leaf
that rattles in the slightest breeze.

I lifted him from behind,
a hand under each arm.
He was light as dead rye

that crumbles underfoot
and lifts into air the way ashes
sprinkled from the brink
of the hill lift with dust
from the land and disappear.

JAMES TREMLETT

Hīnātore*

The fisherman pulls his oars alone.
In the dark star-shimmered harbour the net sparks
blue-white as he hauls, and kahawai struggling
send silent phosphorescent lightning
to the deep. These nights he wearies
with the weight of it, though the kahawai
are few now and hīnātore fading. In distant years
he watched the strong-running schools
shoot sharp swells of light to the far horizon;
as if the body of the water-god
was lit to sudden flame. Tonight
the net brings three only, hardly enough to smoke
but a feed for an old man, and then some.

Across the rivermouth the far red pulse
of the steel mill is sleepless, even now at midnight.
He thinks of his children frantic in the towns
who know no home in this long green land, no stern exertion
of sea or soil; but minds splintered into a thousand fragile shards
and never at peace. No strangeness to them,
that the harbour-bounding hills which are the bones of ancestors
should be chained by pipelines and roads; as if the duress
of the kahawai could teach them nothing.
As if the land were a broken bottle.

It will get worse before the end, he knows.
The fires on the hill-crests burn into the dawn.
The kahawai may leave the harbour altogether,

and he would not blame them. Soon the fisherman too
will not return but pass instead the saltspray curtain
into the long night,
night of the albatross and whale,
and hīnātore take the last of all his debts.

Persistent, a kahawai slaps his leg.
He slips it over the side,
stabs the others behind the eye, and resumes his watch
of sea and sky: his boat an island,
and the earth an island, the stars
like islands overhead. At last
the fisherman straightens, turns his boat
for shore, pulling hard against the tide.
From the unseen lifeline of his wake
the phosphorescence flickers in the night.

---

*   Phosphorescence in the water; stars so distant you cannot see them, only a cloud of light.

Flounder

The old bach was filled with birds and their bones. The dry rustle of their feathers mixed with the sounds of the sea over the mudflats across the road.

Cats probably killed a bunch of them, said Auntie Mel. Or they got trapped in here and starved.

Okay, Mel. No need to be morbid about it or you'll scare the children, said Grandma as she swept small bodies up to a pile in a corner.

'The children' were my three siblings, too many cousins, and myself. We giggled and took some of the birds outside for a miniature funeral before getting into an argument about whether burial or cremation was the right option and giving up.

The bach was falling apart as much as those bird skeletons. Every gust of wind from the bay made it quiver. There were parts of the floor where our biggest uncles, Ted and Pete, couldn't stand because they might fall right through. But we were very lucky to have that old house. Grandma told us every year. She had inherited it from an aunt back in the days when it was not so hard for people to have a bach so close to the sea. The houses and baches around this stretch of sea were all rickety though. Not like those flash ones closer to beaches where there was actually surf and sand. No, this bit of bay was mainly for old fishing boats that settled on the mudflats at low tide. It was one of the last places where normal people, like us (said Grandma), could catch a sea view. Even if the wind did reek of fish guts and rotting algae some days and even if all the shellfish in the area were dying. In the bach's garden, or what we called the garden even though there was no lawn and it mainly grew with broken toys on our once-a-year visits, there was a lonely pōhutukawa tree. Every Christmas, cliché or not, it popped with red from its branches, despite the way we kids carved our names into its bark, despite the stray cats that used it as a scratching post, and despite the sea wind.

This Christmas was like every other Christmas at the bach. Except this time Auntie Mel had finally come back. We kids weren't exactly sure where she was coming back from but we knew she had been away for a long time. And we knew that she was angry. Not angry to be back but angry about whatever had happened when she was away.

Auntie Mel, shooed outside by Grandma who thought being outside might be good for her, walked with us down to the mudflats. The shoreline right before the mudflats was a white highway of broken shells against dark sea-smoothed rocks. All the shells were empty and dead—pipis, scallops, oysters, mussels. Here kids, Auntie Mel said. Let's try to find one with something still inside—like when I was a kid and we went paddling all the time and boiled up the shellfish afterwards for tea.

But we couldn't find any shells with something still alive inside. Auntie Mel was mad about that like she was mad about whatever had happened while she was away. All I knew was that it had something to do with a man down south. Something that made the other women, even Grandma, snap at their husbands and brothers and children to leave Auntie Mel alone and something that kept them up late at night, hands in dishes and knitting, surrounding her like a wall with their bodies. They didn't let any of the rest of us get too close to her. But as I followed Auntie Mel along the shore all I could think was that maybe soon I would be woman enough to stand with her too, my hands deep in dishes.

As the sun started to set and the wind got chillier, we turned our backs to the sea. A cat, perhaps one of the ones that killed all those birds, slunk across the road in front of us. Auntie Mel suggested that we get ice creams from the Pink Shop down the street. We agreed, perhaps too enthusiastically, scared of spooking away her brief moments of good mood. Along the way we stopped to examine the worsening condition of another bach close to ours. This one really was falling apart. The only people we had ever seen there were a couple of homeless people. The grass was halfway up the windows now. A lot of cats had made nests in it. You could take a photo of the yard and play a game to see how many cats you could count and you probably would still not see them all. Every year we wondered if the house would just give up and collapse but here it was, still standing.

We finally arrived at the Pink Shop, a haphazard group of mainly barefoot children all trailing behind Auntie Mel with her long black hair blowing out behind her. The Pink Shop had been there as long as we could remember, as long as the aunties could remember, and as long as Grandma could remember. It only closed on Christmas Day and Easter, and sometimes even on those days Susie who ran it would open if someone were in a particularly dire situation. Such as if someone forgot the matches, even though he promised his wife he had packed them, or if too many children had been in the butter and it was all gone by Christmas lunch. The Pink Shop, like all the buildings along this road, could do with a bit of a paint job, among other things. But it looked like it belonged there, in the orange of the sunset, slowly settling into the bushes that Susie liked to let grow wild.

Auntie Mel let us each pick our own ice cream flavours, instead of making us share like Grandma and Uncle Ted did. The Pink Shop had most things you might need when you are stuck twenty-odd kilometres from the nearest supermarket. Milk of course, but Susie only stocked the whole-fat kind. None of that city-slicker watery stuff, she said. She sold five different ways to light a fire. Plenty of smoking chips in case that fish you just caught needed it. Tinfoil, margarine, a couple of kinds of yoghurt, lollies for the kids. Susie's favourite biscuits, Bell and Twining's teas, peanut butter, and jars of instant coffee. She had cheap white bread and then a couple of loaves of a seeded kind for the tourists. She even had some foil baking pans in case of cooking emergencies, boxes of cereal, and a large amount of oats for porridge. The usual staples.

You're back, said Susie to Mel. Not in a surprised kind of way, but in a matter-of-fact way.

Yes, I guess I am, said Mel. She bought some shampoo along with the ice creams, because Susie happened to have the kind she used.

We took our ice-creams to a picnic table across the road overlooking the receding tide. A man pulled up into the Pink Shop parking spot on a four-wheeler, dragging a trailer filled with giggling small children. All right, everybody off! he yelled. And they all trooped in, presumably to get ice-creams as well, based on their levels of happiness.

The wind had an edge to it, a burn, a feeling that I, over all the Christmases here, connected with feeling food in my belly, the whip of loose clothing and hair, and the knowledge that nothing felt as good as warm after the chill. We complained that we should have brought our jackets but none of us really minded.

When we got back, Uncle Ted and Pete were gearing up for a flounder hunt. The best time to get flounder is in the evenings with the incoming tide. You could spear them out on the mudflats, racing to beat the rising water. But you had to know what you were looking for.

Give us a go, said Auntie Mel.

Yes, give us a go, the rest of us chorused.

The uncles weren't too pleased about this. But, maybe because they didn't want to piss off Auntie Mel, they tossed her a spear and told us older ones to put something on our feet so we could walk over the rocks.

So off we went. An assortment of children, uncles and one aunt, all off to find flounder. We had torches filled with new batteries to spot the fish but most of us only had sticks for spears. It didn't matter. Really we were there for the feeling of it. The feeling of the rocks, slick with slime, through our soggy shoes. The wind getting under our jackets. The flickers of our uncles' torches ahead of us. The thick smell rising up from the water and the mudflats.

Smells like mermaids, whispered Eden, the youngest of the kids who had come out. She probably should have stayed behind. She was only six or something. But Eden had this way of sliding her way into things and she was too soft-spoken and too soft-footed to be a bother.

We flashed our torches all over the mudflats. We saw bottle caps, broken jandals, a few plastic bags, beer cans, some crabs. But no flounder. The uncles got bored and started to pretend they saw things. Above us the stars were becoming all clear. We shivered. The water was warmer than the air but in our now damp clothes the cold was making its way everywhere until we could not feel anything but cold.

Auntie Mel hadn't given up, though. She kept looking for those flounder long after the rest of us devolved into inventing things to stab at in the dark. After a while we thought we should head back to the bach.

We'll make some hot chocolates, said Uncle Pete. See if I can fix the antenna on the TV.

So we all headed back to shore, even Auntie Mel. Our shadows pooled together.

But then—Where's Eden, asked Tina, who was one of the more annoying older cousins and always kept track of everything going on.

Where was Eden? We didn't know. Last time I'd seen her she was crouched over a rockpool, poking sticks into unseen things. Last Uncle Ted had seen her she was rescuing her shoe out of a patch of particularly sticky mud. Last her brother Dean had seen her she was asking too many questions about why flounders are flat, how do they breathe through mud, and why do they like the night time so much. And so on.

None of us were really that worried at first. Except Auntie Mel. She immediately rushed off into the dark, calling Eden's name. Soon all we could see of her was the bouncing light of her torch. We set off with our torches too, but more slowly.

She can't be far, said Uncle Pete. But soon even he didn't sound so sure. The water was rising fast and Auntie Mel's worry began to work its way into us all.

The calls brought out Grandma and the little children and the women who had stayed back at the bach. They kept out of the water but searched the shore, balancing on long concrete pipes left over from another decade. Our calls spread out through the darkness, like night birds taking off.

But we couldn't find Eden.

I decided to catch up with Auntie Mel. I hoped hard that she was the one to find Eden. I didn't think she needed another bad thing going on in her life, whatever the other bad things were, and maybe finding Eden would make her happy for a bit.

When I got to Auntie Mel she was knee deep in water, shaking. Auntie Mel, I said. It's going to be okay. It will be.

I didn't know that for sure. I was afraid too. As if in reply, though, the high voices of two of the smaller boys came across the water from the bach. We found her, we found her! they said. Later on I would find out that the story of Eden going missing had had an anticlimactic ending. She had got tired and returned to the bach, then fallen asleep by the water heater where it was warm and quiet. But right at that moment I was thinking of Auntie Mel's story, and not Eden's any more.

Auntie Mel, I said, almost hip deep in water myself. Hear that? Everything really is okay. She isn't hurt. No one is hurt. Let's go back.

Mel stood and shook. I can't, she said. I can't do it again. It's too hard. All of this. All of it. Too hard. I can't lose another.

In the darkness the water moved. It was Grandma, coming through. Her silhouette met Auntie Mel's in the dark. Yes it is too hard, said Grandma. But you're here. Here at the old bach, and Eden is safe, and we are all safe.

Hold her hands, said Grandma to me and the cousins who had trailed after us. We reached forward, grasping. Then we all walked out of the water together.

When we reached the shore, Auntie Mel did not want to leave the water. There was a deep pool nearby under a tree. Grandma looked at Mel, her eyes just visible in the moonlight, before wading into the pool, clothes and all. Auntie Mel stopped shaking for a second. I felt her under my hands. Then she let go of us and waded into the pool as well. The two women went into the deeper water together. Grandma held Auntie Mel while Auntie Mel cried.

Then one by one, we all went into the deep water too. All of us. Little children, and the old men and aunties who had reached us by this point. Even Eden whose mother had dragged her outside again. The lights from the bach reached out to us from across the road. We children swam around Auntie Mel, combing her skirt and hair with our small fingers. Auntie Mel, Auntie Mel, Auntie Mel, we murmured, and our voices blended with the water and with Auntie Mel's hair and with all her laughter and tears threading out into the dark. Auntie Mel. We were all of us tangled.

JOANNA PRESTON

Swim to Me

Halfway between them—my father's strong hands,
my mother's outstretched arms. The dogs
were hunting on the far side of the river,
and I was learning to swim.

From one pair of sure hands to the other
and back again, face held stiffly up
as I paddled wildly, like the dogs did.

Dad on the black rock in the middle of dark water,
Mum waist deep in the shallows. Halfway between them
when the dogs started barking, and a black snake
arrowed down into the river.

From above, a wedge-tailed eagle
watched the frantic dogs, my parents
frozen as sunlight turned the water
into glass.

The river held me still as death
passed close enough to taste me
on her cloven tongue, the starless dark
of eyes that took me in

and let me go.

The world returns
with Dad shouting my name.

JESS FIEBIG

Maternal Distance

My mother left me at the pier once,
for five hours on a Sunday,
I watched Chinese men gut their fish
in the golden afternoon light,
traced their shadows with the toes of my shoes,
and wondered
        when I would see her again.

I remember her friend colouring
her red hair in our kitchen,
the smell of ammonia
rising from her scalp,
the wet blue slicks of their teeth
from two casks of Velluto Rosso,
the way the silver foils shivered in her hair
as she threw her head back to laugh.

She didn't do that much,
but every now and then spontaneity
tore through her.
Once I found her sitting alone
    at the kitchen table
    blowing bubbles
    in milk through a straw,
giggling as the white froth
spilled over the glass.

She disappeared at Sparks in the Park one year,
I found her passed out
in the back of our old white Corolla,
vomit a collar on her navy woollen jersey
and no way for us to get home.

Life adorned her body;
stretchmarks creeping silver vines
around her abdomen,
freckles on her back from too much time
stoned in the sun,
I used to trace them with my hands.

Bruises bloomed like blue hydrangeas
on her moon-white legs,
a delicate ribbon of broken blood vessels
rose around her neck.

She was quiet, watched half-heartedly,
                from a distance,
                        as I grew.

Mum, I am no longer eleven years old,
gently brushing your amber hair out of those great dark eyes,
asking if you might
                get dressed,
                        go in to work,
                                have something to eat?

Eventually,
I stopped imagining
your soft hands resting on my shoulders,
the warm breath of your whisper.

For years, you would not
look me in the eye,
but I could feel
      your stunted love,
        your gaping sadness,
filling up all the spaces
      between
       us

JESSIE PURU

Taupiri Mountain

it takes away
the sky at night
when you drive past
unable to see its true scale,
and the lights around the royal urupā
substitute the stars—you're driving with people
who don't turn down the music—or slow down to a crawl
then you remember that it isn't a rule—so you acknowledge it with your breath.

you recall
the time people filled this space, from awa to maunga—heaving Te Kuini up to her
final resting place, hī, hā, welcoming her back—raspy breaths expelled—ropes
tightened and formed a path to the top—and the casket floating over the crowd to
take its space as a star.

KIM FULTON

A Campus at Night

We weren't the first to fall in love with Yeats
or drink vodka straight from the bottle here
but perhaps it never occurred to anybody else
to risk a trespass charge to play Chopin,

whose notes rose from the piano in the basement
of the humanities building through empty midnight floors
while outside spring was just beginning
in the same way it always did,
cherry trees blossoming with
the bikes intoxicated boys in rugby jerseys
lodged in their branches.

'We sometimes go there at night,'
a new acquaintance had whispered to me
during an eight o'clock lecture on cell biology.
'The two of us have classical backgrounds,
she plays mean jazz piano.'

I tried to imagine them
diligently practising as children,
thought of the lives we lived before this
moment and would live after
campus security ramped up
and the rugby boys scattered
to office jobs in surrounding cities,
while bikes rested among
fresh foliage, a late summer
breeze catching the wheels,
turning spokes on an axle
this way, then that.

Physics Department

Rumour was he didn't have a university degree
but rode a pushbike across the southern states in the sixties
which was qualification enough to teach the fundamentals
of quantum theory to twenty-five impressionable teens
staring out windows. Nobody knew why
he played the opening credits of *Gilligan's Island*
at the beginning of every class and nobody asked.

We calculated how fast the earth would have to
spin before it propelled us off and what the length
of a day would be. You didn't have to understand
the maths. It asked only a kind of faith
in the man who once worked a suicide hotline.
He said he told a caller who wanted to kill himself
to wash the dishes, which had something to do
with grounding him in the world.
It's good to help others, he concluded. It didn't
take a university education to understand that

physics was no more than the study of
matter and energy—that which occupies
space and its capacity to move. I thought
of his class as I passed the phone booths at
the foot of the Golden Gate Bridge, advertising
crisis counselling for those who had come this
far but hadn't made up their minds yet.
Before he stood at the head of a classroom
spouting stories and expounding equations
he was the voice at the end of a line, a sound
transmitted as signal and wave
and received over a great distance.

RACHAEL TAYLOR

Ground Control

In memory of Ash

It's a modest house on a quiet street in a small hilltop suburb with superb views. We've been here four years now, Jesse, Kyle and me, which is twice as long as any other place we've ever lived. That's four years of pencil scratching height growth with initials on the kitchen doorframe; four years of carpet stains and compost and cupboards packed with obsolescent games and toys. I look out the kitchen window through a frame of pōhutukawa, across a kilometre of houses, out to sea, and I think how lucky I am to have found this place.

The street is home to a range of residents precisely divided. On one side the houses are bought and sold for a million, easy. My side, the houses are on council land. They sit along the edge of two terraced grass playing fields. We're all renters on this side, paying less than you'd expect for similar houses anywhere in the city, and there's a good reason for that.

The primary school my boys attend is situated in the valley, walking distance from our house. It's an Enviroschool. The kids learn about sustainability and kaitiakitanga—guardianship of the land. They help cultivate a community garden on the school grounds and they know all about recycling and ecosystems, environmental footprints; all kinds of information about global warming and climate change. It's as important as knowing your times tables and how to read and spell for this generation who boldly hope to remain living well on planet Earth.

My boys come home with statistics about rubbish decomposition.

'Five hundred years, Mum! That's how long it takes for a plastic bottle to decompose! Same with old nappies. Aluminum cans: two to four hundred years, plastic bags: ten to twenty. Styrofoam: *never*.'

These facts stay with me. 'Two or three months,' I repeat, sweeping autumn's transient waste out the back door. I don't think about these things all the time but probably more than the average person. Maybe it matters more to someone like me because the houses on my side of the street, our house where I'm raising my boys, is built on the edge of a closed landfill. That's what's beneath the cut green grass of the playing fields at the back of our council-owned sections. That's why we pay less to live in this outwardly beautiful and safe area.

Every so often two men from the council enter the back yard where they unlock a silver disc the size of a saucer in the ground and lower their instruments on fine ropes to test the methane gas levels. They wear boilersuits. One's a young man, an apprentice perhaps; the other must be close to retirement age. He talks perpetually in a kind way to the younger, who listens patiently as they carry out their mysterious business. Then they exit through the gate at the back of the property and move about the field unlocking aluminum lids on the large concrete drums, doing their tests, monitoring the site.

Besides these visits there are other conditions to our living here. For example, we're not supposed to smoke, light barbecues or use fireworks—any kind of open flame is prohibited on the grounds and it's spelt out in the tenancy agreement. We can't even use a petrol-powered lawnmower to cut the grass. All these things are fire hazards; the smallest spark could potentially cause a gas explosion.

I did some research before I accepted the terms and conditions of the tenancy. The results don't sound great. Site occupiers at closed landfills are at risk of gas asphyxiation, and toxic and ecotoxic effects from groundwater and soil contaminated by leachate; they may experience injury and infection from exposed objects and refuse. And then there's the chance of landslides, slope failures and the collapse of capped voids. This information is not lost on me.

There's been some land subsidence since we've been here. After a cluster of decent earthquakes a few years back, cracks appeared in the side path and the piles supporting the back end of the house dropped. I contacted our property manager. Official people came with their clipboards and high-vis vests and discussed the situation in low voices, but nothing came of it.

One day I came outside to find Jesse and Kyle digging around the edge of a thick steel H in the ground.

'We're excavating!' said Jesse. 'There's a cavern under here. Look, Mum! It goes down so far.'

'Stop!' I cried. 'What the hell are you doing?'

Their exploratory glee vanished with my overreaction. They were stunned. It was the profile end of a railway I-beam they were digging around. Yes, it could literally go deep. Who knew? Metre upon metre through a hundred years of constantly shifting waste. I was properly upset, but not with them. They didn't know. I was angry at myself for not being able to provide a safer home. What kind of mother was I?

After that I had nightmares: a devastating earthquake left our house (not this one but the house I grew up in) teetering on the edge of a deep rubbish-filled cavern. My childhood bedroom broke off from the rest of the house with me in it and tumbled like a play cube into the ravine. It landed on a jutting ridge and I saw that the cavern was the lair of a monstrous white spider. Aghast, I scrambled to get my bedding back to the main part of the house where I found my boys unconcerned about the quake, the broken house, and the enormous arachnid with which we were now living.

A second dream had me searching desperately for the boys on a vast landfill wasteland. In the distance I could see the eddy and drift of confetti and I was drawn towards it. As I got near I realised it was not confetti but a host of circling black and white gulls. I found the boys there, now part of the landscape of refuse, half buried, their eyes closed and screaming mouths packed with dirt. I'd wake from these nightmares anxious, alarmed. Thankfully, I haven't had those terrible visions in a while.

I've seen people come and go from the street in the time we've been living here, mostly on our side. I've made some friends, too—other mums with kids at the school. There's Jo, a career correspondence student of health and gender studies who also volunteers at a mental health clinic. Jo's an outspoken feminist with a poor opinion of the patriarchy. She's got two kids, a boy, and a girl who identifies as gender fluid. And there's Livi, with her pretty face and paranoia, Jo's opposite. She's strong in her own way but what Livi really wants is a man to love and support her. She wears her heart on her sleeve, gets her hopes up, sleeps with guys on the first date, then, predictably, they disappear. Livi wants a knight but what she gets is arseholes. Rejection inevitably leads to depression and self-medicating. Her seven-year-old daughter, Tuesday, is left to fend for herself, roaming the street looking for company.

'Where's your mum, Tuesday? Does she know where you are?'

'Mum's asleep.' In the afternoon.

'We're about to go out. Go on home now.'

'Where are you going? Can I come? When are you getting back?' she asks.

'Go and check on your mum,' I say, and I watch her through the window zigzag from house to house, knocking on doors, looking for a companion who won't brush her off.

I used to know Lisa before she remarried and moved to our street—across the road. Kyle and her kid were at Playcentre together. She's since had a couple more with her new husband. I tell myself she's busy, preoccupied, it's baby-brain or something. She wears her hair in a conservative way and she's taken out her nose ring. The roller doors on the garage go up and she dashes out in her new SUV; a van delivers groceries to her door. Lisa doesn't remember me now. She's chosen not to.

It's like that with all the women from the other side. They own dogs which they run on the fields behind our houses but they never look over to say hello, and if you happen to be in your back yard or out on the field enjoying the view, the sun, peace and openness, they don't acknowledge you. Instead they call their dogs and children over to the far side of the field or away. Maybe these women think they have more invested—lives they've bought, commitments that are more permanent and consolidated. Whatever the reason, and despite the fact that our kids attend the same school, the women on the side overlooking the valley don't associate with the women from the park side; nor do the women from the park side attempt to befriend those from the view side.

The only time the two sides meet is when we're thrown together under circumstances beyond our control. Once Jo and a woman named Helena reversed their cars into each other as they exited their driveways in a hurry. Helena's car was insured; Jo's was not. It's hard to say who was at fault: each woman blamed the other, both threatened legal action. The damage wasn't much. 'It's the principle,' said Jo. Her car remains dented in on the rear, the bumper askew but still attached.

Livi called Helena an 'Evil'—someone who brings gloom and bad luck wherever they go. She claimed to know some things about her because Tuesday's in the same class as her daughter at school. Apparently Helena's a control freak. Her kid's lunches are gluten-dairy-nut-sugar-free and purely organic; she even has a container of vitamin supplements to swallow at various times throughout the day. Helena doesn't own a cellphone for fear of carcinogenic radiowaves and she shunned the MMR vaccine after reading claims it was linked to autism. According to Livi, Helena had her silver amalgam fillings pulled and replaced with white ones because she believed toxic mercury vapour was passing through her bloodstream, accumulating in her liver and poisoning her. I don't know how Livi knows this except that she's obsessed with teeth because most of hers are rotten and it makes her self-conscious. She's on a waiting list for a government-funded scheme to have them all pulled out and replaced with false ones.

I've seen Helena on the field at times looking distracted and confused. Not walking purposefully for health but wavering. I've wondered about her, but she didn't sound like a particularly nice person and, in keeping with the unspoken rules of the street, I was happy to keep my distance.

Recently I saw her out there with her dog. It was windy, and the gales were blowing her around. There's not much to her—she's bones dressed in designer leisurewear. I was fighting to get the washing pegged on the line. Helena let the dog off its lead and sat on one of the large concrete metal drums, slumped like a pixie on a stone. Dry clumps of cut grass caught on wind currents flew like tiny witches around her. Her dog was bounding up and down the field. She wasn't playing with it or calling to it; she was just sitting there. An Evil, I said to myself.

I finished with the washing and walked up the back steps to the house. I was filling the jug with water for a coffee when Helena's dog came leaping through the open door. It ran excitedly from room to room before I was able to catch it in the kitchen where it had stopped to gobble the cat's food from its plastic dish. Holding the dog's collar, I dragged it towards the back door. Helena hadn't even noticed her pet was missing.

'Hey,' I yelled, 'your dog just ran through my house!'

Helena looked at me. She called the dog but it didn't respond. It had broken free of my hold and was snuffling around a gap under the house. Helena made her way across the field, through the gate and the overgrown grass, into my property. She didn't apologise for the canine intrusion.

'Chiot! What a naughty dog,' she said to it.

'What's it called again?' I asked.

'Chiot. It's French for puppy,' Helena said.

I couldn't help wondering at her choice of name, having heard her sometimes, exasperated, desperately calling the disobedient dog's name like a profanity across the field.

Helena looked to be in a bad way. Her hair, wrapped in a scarf, was coming unravelled and when her sunglasses fell from her face with the movements of the heaving animal I saw that she'd been crying.

'I was just putting the jug on,' I said. 'Would you like a cup of tea or coffee?'

'No, I don't think so.'

'It's no trouble.' I took hold of the leash and looped it around the metal handrail by the steps. 'Chiot: sit!' I said, and the dog did as it was told.

Helena was disoriented. She followed me into the house, remarking that the dog had never taken to her ... it had been her husband Andrew's idea ... for protection and for company because he was often away from home, but she'd never liked the dog.

'An albatross around my neck,' she said. The dog had failed its obedience training. Branded 'an emphatically unmanageable creature', it was soon to be rehomed.

I handed her a cup of coffee. Helena looked from the white plastic jug stained yellow at the spout to the sink full of unwashed dishes, to the filter-less taps, to the cup in her hand, chipped on the rim and its black filmy contents. She placed it warily on the bench and didn't touch it again.

She continued to talk, though, about her husband. She never said outright what the problem was but I got the idea. I thought about my own ongoing trials with my boys' dad, but that was different again. Helena was voicing advice to herself; she already knew the answer, only she wished she didn't.

'You can either put up with it,' she said, as she had done for so long, 'or you can say no, I'm not prepared to do this any longer and make a change. Simple.' But she backtracked when I agreed.

'Divorce?' she said. 'That's out of the question.'

She'd been on the verge of leaving her husband before, but she admitted frankly that she'd never survive without his income. She didn't want to have to work full time and raise her daughter, and she certainly couldn't go on a benefit. She'd be despised and scorned, rejected by her friends and peers. Andrew was some public-sector CEO. (When I related the incident to Jo later she said, 'Those fuckers are the biggest beneficiaries of all. They get paid shitloads and it's all on the taxpayer.')

'It's not so bad, solo parenting, you know,' I said.

'My God,' said Helena, 'are you kidding me? How can you be satisfied with this?' She gestured incredulously at the room. 'Living this way? No husband, no prospects, no money or nice things?'

'I'm happy,' I said, stunned by her insensitivity, tears forming against my will.

'Oh, I get it,' she said, like she had me figured out. 'You've got nothing to lose.'

We stood around the wooden steps at the back door in the early evening, me, Jo and Livi, smoking rollies.

'That bitch,' Jo said. 'She deserves to stay with her cheater husband in their toxic marriage.' We laughed at the irony of it. 'How dare she say those things to you!' Jo had a way of setting the world straight. Weren't my circumstances, those that united me with Livi and Jo and left me at odds with the likes of Helena, beyond my control? Helena would never change or understand a different perspective; it would be a waste of time even trying. I had my own problems. Helena was best left alone.

It had been a strange and emotional day and I said so.

'That's why. A full moon,' said Livi, pointing to the yellow globe as it bellied out from behind the Norfolk pine.

'So true. If you ever doubt the effect of a full moon come visit me at the mental health centre,' said Jo.

'Oh, I believe it,' I said. 'I'll happily take that for an excuse.'

After the women had left and the boys were camping in the lounge on mattresses dragged from their bedroom, I returned to the yard, drawn by the luminescent otherworldly atmosphere of the night. The northerly wind of the day had dropped but a mild breeze animated the night garden. Tea-towels left out danced on the line; the copper-red golden-red leaves of the neighbouring ash tree quivered like sequins and fluttered to the ground. Even with the back-door light on the amber stars looked too bright: autumnal, unnatural in the night sky like they might blow down too. A night like this made you wonder.

I wanted time to freeze, so I could hold on to something lasting, be sure of something. I needed reassurance that everything would be okay.

Jesse appeared and sat beside me on the step. He complained about Kyle calling him a stupid baby. He didn't want to be alone, his older brother ignoring him with his headphones on.

'You want to shish on a star tonight?' I said. That's the way Jesse used to say it when he was little, and it stuck, something to smile at. 'Look at the moon. It's big tonight, huh?'

'I'm making a wish, Mum.'

'You know, men have travelled to the moon in spaceships. Can you believe that?'

'I know that already. We learnt about it at school,' said Jesse.

To be honest I struggled to comprehend that astronauts landed a spacecraft on the moon nearly fifty years ago, bounced around for a few hours *and* returned safely to Earth to tell about it. (Livi thinks the moon landing's a conspiracy. She's convinced it was filmed in a studio in Arizona by Stanley Kubrick, no less.) But of course Jesse believes it. It's easy for a child to believe in possibility and I'm grateful for that.

Jesse's my dreamer. It's Kyle I worry about. He's the man of the house, still only ten. Knower of things he shouldn't be burdened with, like our money problems. He feels responsible. I know it troubles him as he develops his understanding of disappointment and loss. I can't afford to give him the things his friends and peers have. It's shaping his sense of male identity: men are the builders of the world, of civilisation, the makers of history. He thinks women are weak, and resents me for being here for him. I'm not his father. But Kyle's a child, he doesn't fully understand.

The thing is, Lenny, the boys' dad, struggles with addiction. He's been in and out of detox and rehab centres for years. He's still around, sometimes more often than I'd like, but I allow it for the boys' sake. They love his energy; his fun-dad tactics; the sugar, junk food and noise; the 'maleness' I simply can't provide. The problem is consistency. Lenny can't hold anything down. Employment's sporadic (painting houses for a mate's business, usually). His wages are spent on his habit. He'll disappear for days or weeks at a time: unreachable.

Lenny's never had a permanent place to live, either, so having the boys to stay was never an option until recently. He's been clean a while this time. He's been working, and he's got himself a two-bedroom flat. Social Services checked it out and reported it's suitable for the boys to stay overnight on a regular basis. I try to look at the positive aspects of them spending more time with their dad, the prospect of having some time to myself, but what I really feel is fear. All I've built and worked towards and secured is coming undone.

Lenny and I agreed on one night, just as a starter, not only for him and the boys but for me. Kyle and Jesse are my whole life. Caring for them keeps me grounded. It's not just the loss of companionship but of purpose and control. There's a madness that comes over a person without it.

'I'm here, and I'm a constant,' I said quietly now to Jesse. 'We have a happy home, we do. We've got each other.'

'Maam, stop.' I was holding him so tight he complained and said he was going back inside.

It's hard raising kids on your own—there's no one to carry you. Me, Jo, Livi ... We fall short, mess up, pick up the pieces, rinse and repeat. We all do the best we can.

I spent that day they were gone cleaning—the shower, the skirting boards, the oven, even the utensil drawers where crumbs and grime accumulate in the curved valleys of the cutlery tray.

In the boys' room I stripped the sheets from the bunks and tucked in fresh ones but not before holding the old pile to my face and inhaling the buttery biscuit smell of the linen. I vacuumed and dusted the window ledges and shelves littered with Jesse's collections of found stuff—sticks and rocks, bits of metal, broken pens, shells and sea glass. I recognised some element of treasure in these items, the fact that these were chosen while other objects were not. There's logic to this chaos within the parameters of Jesse's imagination. Meanwhile, Kyle collects empty soda bottles and displays them proudly like anti-trophies. There are things I can't control in my own children and I'll just have to learn to accept that.

I sat on the bedroom floor beside the vacuum cleaner and messaged Lenny.

'Everything okay?'

'☺☺ Just battling two tired boys and one shower bahahaha Made a huge meal All Jesse ate was apple and bbq sauce FML'

'He's always been a fussy eater. I can pick them up earlier tomorrow if you want?'

'Nah all goods Got some work on but cant be assed ;) Gimme 30 min to get these toads sorted and they can call u back'

'It's ok. Just tell them goodnight from me.'

The contact did little to ease my mind. I walked through the house and only noticed the futility of my actions—a whole day spent cleaning and still autumn leaves had found their way inside; dust and cobwebs clotted neglected corners. Where was the pause button? What was the point of all this?

I stood on the back steps and viewed the field beyond the yard, a wide-striped mown pattern. The night was still and desolate blue under that faraway rock, the moon. I considered the ragged remains of Jesse's homework project bird feeder hanging from a ghostly branch of the ash tree. It was a pinecone iced with peanut butter. The birds never did fall for it, but it had survived a surprisingly long time, sticky with sinister promise on its rotting core.

Around eight a knock sounded on the front door. I was startled by its clumsy and urgent rhythm. Still thinking about my boys and fearing the worst, I ran to answer it. Helena fell inside. It was about a month since our last encounter. She crawled over the mat and lay on the carpet crying dramatically. Her face was stained with makeup, dark around the eyes. Andrew had locked her out of the house—she'd been drinking and had confronted him about his infidelity. This was the gist of it. Her heaving and sobbing distorted the story. I knelt down to hold her, and she cried a big wet patch into the front of my T-shirt.

Eventually Helena wore herself out. Carefully, I helped her stand, and guided her into the boys' room, where I tucked her in on the bottom bunk and sat beside her with a tentative hand on her shoulder. It was a relief to comfort her, grown woman though she was. This awful woman who'd insulted me and judged me was now helpless and rejected; she needed me. In this moment we needed each other.

'Don't you *dare* feel sorry for me, don't you *ever*,' she slurred quietly.

I shook my head, looked at her shrivelled hand heavy with jewellery clutching the top of the duvet, her eyes tweaking behind closed lids. But I did feel sorry for her all the same.

Helena's fretting ceased, and she slept. I left her side, crossed the road to her house and knocked on the door. Helena's husband didn't invite me inside. He seemed irritated, as though he'd been interrupted by an unwanted salesperson.

'She was pretty upset but she's sleeping it off. I don't mind if she stays,' I said. 'My kids are away this weekend. I just wanted to let you know where she is and that she's okay.'

He didn't seem to care either way.

'Okay,' I said. 'Just thought you should know.'

He shut the door. I went home, checked on Helena, quiet now and small as a child. I went to bed.

The next morning she was gone. Perhaps she'd left during the night. I stood at the back door watching the sky lighten behind the houses on the far side of the field. The angle of the rising sun cast long calligraphic shadows onto the field from young pōhutukawa growing along its edge. I was relieved to see the new day. I'd slept poorly, my mind swarming with dreams and anxious thoughts, encores and variations of visions from my subconscious past. It warmed me to know that Kyle and Jesse would be back home by lunchtime. They would again occupy and direct my thoughts and movements.

I waited a few days before calling on Helena, who greeted me with few words. I suppose I, as part of the entire embarrassing incident, was best erased from memory. Helena had somehow 'fallen' to the other side of the street and she felt certain in retrospect that I was part of the reason for that, rather than the provider of a safe refuge, her maternal nurturer on her dreadful night. She didn't know how to apologise or even acknowledge me under such circumstances so she made excuses—she must have been having a bad reaction to a new medication. Things were fine between her and Andrew. All couples have their 'moments'. They were putting the house on the market, making a new start. She could never be well as long as they lived this close to a closed landfill, and in this awful mercurial climate, et cetera.

I must have looked doubtful.

'I've been married seventeen years,' she said. 'Don't you look at me like that. You don't know what it takes to a make a marriage work, the sacrifice a woman makes.'

I thought of Lenny and the struggles I'd had with him over the years, trying my best to raise the boys. Every new phase, the trouble it took to stay adaptable to change. But that was a whole different story. I had no idea what it was like to be Helena. We were not the same. The collision of our lives was only circumstantial, involuntary. This would be the last time we'd meet.

Leaving Helena's property, I walked into the middle of the street and turned south towards the view. The sky was violet and low to the east a heavy moon was waning. Winter would be here soon. It would come without warning.

red suitcase

the novelty wore off fast
we hunkered down in an
old prison in Fremantle
not operational but
stalked by wandering souls

mary who was hanged
juniper who
hid under floorboards and
almost burrowed his way to freedom

in all this
tugging of conscience
you said
you were not coming back
your stepfather was enraged
not realising his heart
had fallen inwards

you my brave girl
held your clear gaze

your suitcase
redder than a war poppy
chose that same moment
to offer up
its handle
feeling the strain
it just snapped off

Do You Know My Poetry?

1. 'Do you know my poetry?' asks Johnny Depp playing William Blake in Jim
   Jarmusch's surreal western movie *Dead Man*. Johnny is not William Blake
   the poet but another Blake & the joke is that a helpful Indian called
   Nobody (who likes to recite the real WB) thinks he is the poet. This
   namesake Blake is dying of a gunshot wound & makes that inquiry above,
   just before he kills two US marshalls who are tracking him for a murder
   he didn't commit. *Bang! Bang!* goes the irony.

2. Poetry is a queer profession. Even a gentle confession of love wants to
   travel like a bullet. What poet wouldn't want to kill the world that turns
   its back on truth? The poet thinks: 'But, wait—there's more'—quite
   possibly a pack of lies, from deep down where the gadoid fish swim, or a
   brewed fake elixir—just worthy of hawking at some tawdry fairground of
   ears.

3. It's tricky when the morning task is to shave the pain off your face, but
   the mind is trapped in the sound of raindrop percussion on a tin roof.
   You might gasp at the battery of tiny ghosts come to visit. Your fingers
   might become a banjo strumming against the shitty weather. It slowly
   sinks in that you're involved in a problem that can never be resolved.

4. It was just a teeny text: *I want to be either horizontal or be drinking nice Merlot.*
   She became an obsession—a little like dancing on a staircase. I slowly
   became unzipped & looked up the meaning of 'bats in the belfry'. In my
   dream, we lived in a cave, with the Nazis on horseback outside. I was
   having a lot of cave-dreams at that time. They said Osama bin Laden was
   living in one.

5. I walked the Grey Lynn streets, chugging Crest beer. I laughed at a smoky VW Bug with a Greenpeace sticker, farting like bad sax. Unemployment had never felt so good. At home, through a crack in the curtain, workers moved in heavy syrup. I watched a lot of CNN & fell in love with the beauty of burning oil wells. The firefighters drank Castrol GTX & raised their dirt-encrusted mattocks to the sky.

6. You were supposed to learn the rules & then throw them away. The original idea of sticking it up the bourgeoisie was good. I told the children to put down their pencils & run around outside in the rain. Their voices carried higher than the cubic geometry of the city. I called it like I saw'd it. I told them that the sky came all the way down to the ground.

RUSS FLATT

Untitled

1. *Ever*, 2016, 841 x 1189 mm.
2. *Half A Person*, 2015, 1016 x 1016 mm.
3. *Shorts, Not Undies*, 2015, 594 x 840 mm.
4. *Snap*, 2013, 762 x 1143 mm.
5. *Swimming Pool #3*, 2013, 730 x 910 mm.
6. *Untitled #2*, 2014, 640 x 1000 mm.
7. *Untitled #3*, 2014, 640 x 1000 mm.
8. *Untitled #4*, 2014, 640 x 1000 mm.

All works are inkjet photographs on Hahnemühle Photo Rag and editions of 3 plus 1 AP.
Courtesy the artist and Tim Melville Gallery: www.timmelville.com

Growing up gay in suburban Auckland during the 70s and 80s wasn't easy. There were few 'out' role models, so gay people were conditioned to lead private, secret and sometimes double lives. In mainstream news the mention of anything gay was usually AIDS-related, so sexual connections were shrouded in death and danger. There was the ever-present fear of being infected with the virus, as well as of being arrested by police or attacked by homophobic bullies. It is sometimes stressful to recall these experiences as an adult; and as memories shift over time, one is left wondering whether 'memory' is a reality or simply an abstract idea.

The memories I reconstruct in my photographs have helped me to acknowledge and process my subconscious grief. And to my delight, these images also operate as celebrations of heroes we have lost and journeys we have taken. The fighting, the marching, and the relentless protesting by brothers and sisters who went before us mean that today I can get married, foster a child with my husband, and have (almost) the same legal rights as a heterosexual citizen. Furthermore, thanks to gay activist pressure on pharmaceutical companies, HIV is no longer a death sentence.

—Russ Flatt

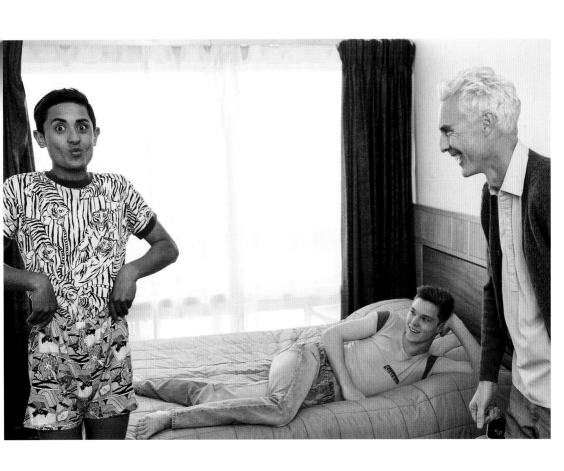

JOSEPH BARBON

The Joy of Overrating

We mostly say we like art for its power over us and mostly mean we like art for our power over it. For every encounter with the sublime there are fifty-odd works where our pleasure's all in the classification: where we rank it, how we square it with our values, how we establish ourselves in the cultural conversation. If we aren't willing to cop to adolescent list-making or comment-prepping, we can at least all remember seeing someone's eyes light up when the conversation drifts the right way and they have their chance to say 'Never thought much of Bellow—a hack, if you ask me' or 'X-Men 2— defining cultural document of our young century, I reckon'.

Obviously that's the 'bad' way to enjoy art, but when most of us make just a few meaningful decisions in our lives, who'd be priggish enough to deny anyone the play-agency of reducing someone's years of work to a quip? If art has any objective social benefit, it's facilitating criticism, which is fun, free, and provides a harmless outlet for the aggression of innumerable cranks.

But unfairly knocking something is small-time—the real fun's in unfairly praising it. For one, your power as a consumer is much greater; when you criticise something, you're in combat with it and might lose, but when you're elevating it, it's helpless. You're declaring the victory of your critical sensibility over the facts. You identify with the artist but you're also above them, gift-bestowing, godlike. It's the most meaningless power-trip imaginable, and therefore the most pure. It's rebellious in a nicely trivial way—you're committing a critical crime, distorting a work's 'real' reception. It feels like you're forging a document or vandalising something. But it's a victimless crime—you might waste someone's time, sure, but they'd get enough pleasure out of disagreeing with you to make up for it. And you're a heroic outlaw, dutiful, knightlike, saviourish. *Seven Samurai* doesn't need your help, but who's going to give *Judo Saga* any love unless you step in and pretend to like it?

A really good bit of overpraise tells a story, suggests a whole perverse value system. Obviously there's no fun calling *Lolita* the greatest novel ever written, since you might really mean it. Much better is calling Rod Stewart's *Never a Dull Moment* the key record of the 1970s. You want something with intensity but a narrow range—a scared-straight drug novel, say, or an especially melancholic sixties girl group. Something with clear edges that feels comfortable reduced to a piece of rhetoric, something you know won't get away on you.

Masochists, according to pop-Freud, like to partner with pushovers and play helpless thrall to someone they really have full control over. My pathology towards art is about the same. I once insisted everyone I knew see *Hot Blood*, an unremarkable, presumably offensive Nicholas Ray film whose lead character is described on Wikipedia simply as 'a sexy gypsy'. I liked it mostly because there was lots of red in it and you didn't have to follow the plot too closely, but performed overwhelmedness anyway; I said the movie was the fullest expression of Ray's themes and the highest possible melodrama and pretended it put me in one of those trances Wagner fans were meant to go into (they were probably faking too).

Why *Hot Blood*? I liked what it said about me, obviously—I assumed my appreciation of its idiot Salammbô sensualism would suggest a multi-layered irony and zest for the tawdry that would win me the love and respect of my peers. It didn't, but that's not important, because the value of overrating something is personal. It's an ego-strengthening exercise, an assertion of the value of your own ignorant experience against the wisdom of consensus.

We're hit every day with a thousand deligitimisations of our lives, our joys. The utopias of pleasure we imagine others can get to is phony, so why shouldn't we make up sublime pleasures of our own? When we say the Linton dairy does the best fish and chips in the country, it makes them taste better and doesn't hurt anyone. Isn't saying *Flowers in the Attic* is better than *To the Lighthouse* the same thing?

Overrating is one of the only cultural weapons the province has against the centre, and as a provincial nation we need every defence we can get, and as a miserable nation we need every thrill we can get, and to say in cheerful bad faith that the pleasures we can access and control are the best ones of all is one of the best ones of all.

Fish-tank Lightbulb

He wasn't as charming as a catfish or a guppie, but we were all pretty gutted when Sam the goldfish died. It didn't matter that he was dull as a plank. In my house, we don't devalue boring things. Otherwise there'd be nothing to stop us carpet-bombing every town between here and Auckland.

Carlos bought Sam the goldfish from the pet shop in town, back when we first hooked up. I remember watching from the kitchen window as he parked his truck by the back door and pulled the fish tank from the passenger seat. He had an air pump and some oxygen weed, aquarium pebbles, a long fluorescent light and a goldfish swimming in a plastic bag. He struggled to carry it all up the steps, still wearing his work boots and hi-vis vest.

Carlos said the goldfish was a present for my wee boy Layne, a way for the two of them to bond. Layne can be pretty shy, y'know? You need something to get him chatting. And it worked, too—him and Carlos got on like a house on fire, and this time there was no 'You're not my real dad'.

But eventually Sam did what all goldfish do—he died. We lost a lot of goldfish that year. When Layne heard about it, he said, 'I reckon Sam deserves a proper burial, don't you, Mum?' Yep, he actually said that. He sounded just like Carlos too, slight Māori accent and everything. So the two of them got some little decorations and the box from a packet of king-size matches, and made a little funeral tray for Sam.

When they were finished, Layne frowned and shook his head. 'It's too sad,' he said. 'It needs more colour, it should be happy.' And he was right. Carlos was great with fish-tank logistics, but he couldn't design a funeral arrangement to save himself. Which is crazy, cos he's had plenty of chances to learn. This is Whanganui—everyone fucking dies here.

Carlos said, 'Too right, mate. More colour, I reckon.' He said that Sam deserved something special for his funeral tray. He was part of the family. That means something. And a funeral should be a celebration, and not so bloody sad. I looked around the bathroom for that special little touch to lay beside Sam's body and make his funeral tray come to life.

'Ah ha!' I said, 'I know just the thing.' I delicately and respectfully reached over and picked up a bright pink hair tie.

'Babe, did you just pull that out of the rubbish bin?'

'It doesn't matter where it came from.'

'Jesus, Jem. It's still got your hair on it.'

'It's fine,' I whispered. 'He's just a bloody fish.'

Mistaaaaake.

'He was *not* "just a fish",' Carlos said. 'He was a mate of ours. And now he's gone.'

Layne started to sniffle, and I eyeballed Carlos, hard.

Carlos put his hand on Layne's shoulder. 'It's okay, mate. Sometimes we love people and then we lose them. That's life. We just need to remember the good things and be thankful for the times we had.'

I rolled my eyes. Honestly, sometimes Carlos can be a bit cringe. But he stayed with me through the relapses, so I let certain things slide.

Carlos made us all take turns telling stories about Sam. Y'know, stuff like 'Sam was a loyal friend', 'Sam was not a stupid fish', and 'Sam could understand every word we said, but he was an independent-minded little bugger so he refused to sit and heel and do backflips'. It was all bullshit, of course. Well-intentioned bullshit, but bullshit nonetheless. Sam was a fundamentally boring fish.

I ruffled Layne's hair. 'Time to say goodbye, mate. Do you wanna do the honours?'

Layne nodded his little head, then leaned forward and pressed the smaller of the two buttons on top of the toilet. And as the water poured into the bowl and overturned his funeral tray, I thought three things:

One, Carlos was right, funerals *should* be celebrations.

Two, you don't know how much you'll miss someone until they're gone. Like, I never gave two shits for Sam when he was alive, but standing there next to the bowl, thinking of the bulb lighting an empty fish tank, it was all too much.

And third and finally, when flushing the floating carcass of a goldfish, you definitely need to press the big button.

Later that evening, after I'd tucked Layne into bed, I came back into the kitchen. Carlos was putting away the dishes with a tea-towel slung over his shoulder. 'You get him down all right?' he asked.

'Yeah-nah, he was okay, all things considered.'

'Yeah. Rough day for the wee fulla. Well, I suppose we'd better take him into town this weekend, ay? Go pick another goldfish.'

I was stunned. 'Good god no. I don't wanna put him through that again.'

'Why not? That's life, things die. Kids need to learn that early. And goldfish are better than puppies, they die sooner.'

'Jesus Christ, are you serious?'

'Yeah, sure. What's wrong with that?'

'It's a bit bloody morbid, isn't it? He's gonna learn about death eventually, we don't need to rush it.'

Carlos shook the tea-towel out and hung it on the oven door. 'It's better to be honest with kids about stuff like this,' he said. 'You don't have to come, me and him can go in together.' And then he gave me that look of his, the one that said, 'after all I've done for you', and there's not much I can say to that. So off we went to Donald's Pet Emporium to get another goldfish.

This next goldfish was called Bubble and he was a 'Calico Shubunkin', which is pet shop language for splotchy and bug-eyed. Now, Layne is a kind and gentle little fella and I love him to bits, but let's face it—he can't spell for shit. That's how Bubble's name changed to Buble, like the singer. The new name fitted him pretty well cos, like Michael Bublé, the new goldfish was plain and bug-eyed and, despite his many talents, he was *really* boring. In fact, Bublé the fish was so much like Bublé the singer that I considered buying a little piano for the fish tank. But in the end I thought, nah, you don't get a reward for being dull. As a parent, you learn to not incentivise bad behaviour.

Anyway, Bublé the goldfish lasted four or five weeks before he too ended up on a decorated tray in the toilet bowl. At this stage I wasn't worried. An old fish dies, so you get a new one. Then the new one dies—sometimes you get a dud. It happens. Just tell Layne it's not his fault, then press the big button on the dunny.

But not long after, Layne started having bad dreams and asking awkward questions about goldfish heaven. I was ready to give up on goldfish entirely but Carlos said, 'We just need to find the right fish. We've had a run of bad luck, sure, but it's important for kids to learn about responsibility and mortality.'

I put my hand on his arm. 'Babe, I think he's got the mortality bit.'

Carlos secretly agreed, I think, but he wouldn't budge. And that's how we ended up with a goldfish that neither of us really wanted, named Christopher Weiland-Bennington. I came up with the name for this one. The rock stars Chester Bennington, Chris Cornell and Scott Weiland had all just died, so I thought it'd be a nice tribute. In hindsight, naming a goldfish after two suicides and an overdose may have been tempting fate.

Anyway, Layne was pretty worried about Mr Weiland-Bennington right from the start. He started having bad dreams, and I caught him googling 'how to keep a goldfish alive'. He read that fish like having a hiding place, so we bought a little fish-tank schoolhouse for Weiland-Bennington to hide in.

We weren't taking any chances this time. We'd been burnt twice by those flimsy little bastards, so I tried to stop Layne from getting too attached. I told him that, quite frankly, I didn't trust Christopher Weiland-Bennington. He looked shifty. He swam like he had something to hide. The way he wiggled his tail seemed snobby and rude, and also completely unoriginal. I put my face to the glass and said, 'Mate, get over yourself. You're a goldfish. You're not that cool.'

I told Layne that, just by looking at him, you knew Christopher Weiland-Bennington was a bigot. The type of goldfish who'd say things like, 'I'm not a racist, I'm a race realist.' The type of goldfish who'd blame women and immigrants for low wages. The type of goldfish who'd say, with a straight face, 'Slavery was better for black people because slave owners had an incentive to care for their property.'

When I told Carlos about the goldfish's views on the Treaty of Waitangi, he shook his head in disbelief. 'We expected this from Bublé—but not from you, Christopher,' he said. 'Not from you.'

I put my hand on Layne's shoulder. 'You can't trust goldfish. The little buggers will drop dead out of sheer hatred.'

And soon enough, the little hate-monger was dead. Layne found him tanning his belly under the light, with fuzzy grey fungus growing on his side.

We scooped him up and told Layne, 'Don't cry for him, mate. He was the literal Hitler of goldfishes.'

There was no ceremony this time. Just one flush and, despite our best efforts, a few tears from Layne. But his nightmares got worse and then, eventually, it happened.

It was just after midnight on a Tuesday when Layne yelled out from his bedroom. Another bad dream. I went in and gave him a cuddle and tucked him back into bed. As I was about to leave, he asked, 'Mum, does everyone die?'

I cleared my throat. 'Well, eventually, yeah. But not for a long time. And people live a lot longer than fish. So don't worry, okay?'

'Okay.'

Phew.

'Mum?' He said.

'Yeah, mate?'

'How did Dad die?'

I thought, Fucking Carlos and his lessons on mortality.

'I'll tell you when you're older,' I said. 'It's complicated. Now you better get some sleep, ay.'

'Can you leave the hallway light on?'

'Yeah, sure thing. Sleep tight, okay? And don't worry about that stuff.'

When I got back to bed I told what Carlos what happened.

'That bloody pet shop,' he said. 'This is all their fault.'

'Mate, it was your idea.'

'How was I to know we'd lose three in two months? They're supposed to live for five to ten years.'

'Well, now Layne is asking how Brian died,' I said. 'So that's it, no more goldfish.'

'Fine,' said Carlos. 'But I'm going to the pet shop to get our money back and give that cunt a piece of my mind.'

So the next day we went back into Donald's Pet Emporium and spoke to the man behind the counter. 'Mate, you're selling us sub-par goldfish,' I said.

He snickered and said, 'Actually, sub-par is a good thing. In golf, the scoring system—'

'Oh, fuck off,' said Carlos. 'Look, we got him a pet because we wanted to teach him that death is *part* of life, not bloody *all* of it.'

I turned to Carlos. '*You* wanted to teach him that. I was quite happy leaving it alone.'

The guy at the pet shop asked a bunch of questions about pH levels and water salinity. He seemed genuinely confused about the fish dying, which I refused to believe. How can anyone who deals in tropical fish be surprised by death?

Eventually the manager came out and scooped their plainest orange goldfish into a clear plastic bag. 'Just go with a common goldfish,' he said. 'They're basically bulletproof.'

'We don't want another goldfish, we want our money back.'

From behind us, Layne said, 'I want another goldfish.'

'Nah, mate. How 'bout we give the goldfish a break for a while, ay?'

'But I want another one. I don't want an empty tank in my room.'

The manager held out the plastic bag. 'Go on. Free of charge.'

Carlos looked at me, and then turned to Layne. 'Come on, mate, let's go look at the puppies. We'll leave Mum to talk to the man.'

When Layne was out of sight, I sighed and grabbed the bag. 'All right, but this one better last.'

I took the bag over to Layne and held it out. 'I've had a chat with the pet shop man, and he reckons this is the roughest, toughest goldfish they've got. They had to keep him a special tank cos he keeps eating the others and head-butting the glass.'

Layne smiled.

'I'm not kidding! This fella is dangerous. Donald said that if a nuclear bomb goes off, the only things to survive will be cockroaches, old Nokia phones, and this little guy here.'

Layne's eyes widened. He grabbed the bag.

When we got home we put the goldfish in the tank and watched it swim straight for the little schoolhouse.

'What do ya reckon we name this fulla?' said Carlos.

Layne gently tapped on the glass. 'Gohan the goldfish,' he said.

Carlos and I looked at each other and nodded. A *Dragon Ball Z* character. That's how you know you've raised a kid right.

Later that evening, when I went in to kiss Layne goodnight, I stood in the hallway and listened to him talking to his new mate. 'You're the toughest fish ever,' he said. 'Way tougher than those other dumb ones.'

I thought, moments like these make you almost glad you had kids. These little unguarded moments where they're doing the right thing, without threats or bribes.

From the hallway I heard Layne say, 'I know tough fishes don't need a kiss goodnight, but you're getting one anyway.'

I peeked around the corner and saw Gohan the goldfish wriggling in Layne's fist. Layne kissed him once on each side and once on the face, then dropped him back into the water.

As I tucked Layne into bed I glanced over at Gohan. He was spasming on his side and slowly floating up towards the surface, turning and raising his belly and twitching his final twitches. I kissed Layne goodnight, then tiptoed over to the fish tank and flicked off the light.

DEREK SCHULZ

Secrets

I knew a man, who knew a man, who knew a locksmith
—Janet Frame

Janet Frame's *The Lagoon and Other Stories* is a mid-century book, issued, my edition says, in 1951, the year following my birth. The design is classic Caxton Press. Handsome yet homely, it rests on the palm as a testament to the publisher's idealism and attention to detail. The form and script look back to socialist pamphlets of the 1930s, while the graphic on the paper cover (which has the texture of luncheon wrap) anticipates mid-fifties Modern. Yet even the typos, of which there are many, seem determinedly placed to undermine the middle-class values that were taking a hold on the culture. They serve to keep the reader on guard and grounded. But this is not a modern book and these are not modern stories, and there is one here that is a masterwork—'The Secret'.

Though set twenty years before my time, these early stories arouse a deep nostalgia. They call up the domestic life of a South Island childhood with its washhouse and tubs, the hand wringer through which umpteen flannelette sheets were wrung (*twice*) on Mondays; then also the wayward threads of childhood conspiracies hatched in a sandhill thicket or pine plantation where a sensuous curiosity was growing heady on the scent of lupin flower.

And again, the blunt edge of a southern dialect that spilled out the brusque slang of 'bowser', 'dozo' and 'slushy', with phrases to match—'shag-bags' and 'hell's teeth', then the conversation closing—'I'll see you *when on*'.

The stories are constructed in fragments, images that emerge as scenes from the movies the author romances, notes taken on a sudden flight that inexplicably stop, or meditations on writing that read like doodles but are not, for the reader travels along confluent lines of language that are sabotaged in the most unexpected ways. The mind at work here is mature and compelling, the writing precociously girlish and gruelling, for it harbours a dark wit that can move with disarming nervy confidence from the quirky to the sublime to the searingly sly. Into this brew her characters might find themselves unexpectedly dipped.

'The girls looked like lollies and when they turned to us and smiled shy smiles, they looked like little pink lollies waiting to be licked.'

This is from 'My Cousins Who Could Eat Cooked Turnips', an account of railway children meeting stuffy cousins who turn out to be okay, though the admission remains qualified, for the story cannot rid itself of the jealousy it feels toward the cousins' relative affluence, nor its distaste for the hoity pose the characters adopt, feeling obliged in the end to swing them off as 'high as a dunny rose'.

There is an authorial apartness here that the writing cannot hide. It signals a sharp, competitive complexity that sits hand in hand with a governing isolation Frame rarely admits and cannot manage—a lonely, superior, embattled puzzlement that deepens the work immeasurably wherever she attempts to approach it.

And this she does in 'The Secret', a subtle, confabulating and increasingly dangerous lie by which she attempts to approach an appalling truth.

In a family of sisters caught up in a shared desperation, a fantasy world of writing seems a gift, a naturally complicit conspiracy of escape. The Brontës provide the model, a circumstance Frame acknowledges in an early memoir, Beginnings ...

'With a background of poverty, drunkenness, attempted murder and near madness it was inevitable that we should feel close to the Brontës,' she recalls, signalling that she felt herself to be Charlotte, with a responsibility to foster the well-being of her younger siblings. But it is in the desperate interior landscapes of Emily that she found herself increasingly marooned, and soon abandoned the role of mentor to concentrate her attention on the full-time business of writing herself away from them.

She had lost two sisters to tragedy, and it is in the measuring of these disasters that 'The Secret' concentrates its steely puzzlement.

The narrator is Nini, a name that seems conjured from ninny, a term of childhood insult denoting foolishness, and taken from a common phrase describing the way a weaned child might continue to suck at a thumb or blanket in substitute for a mother's breast. There is sensuous pleasure in it, comfort in times of crisis, but also shame, for it marks a refusal to leave childhood behind. And so it becomes a secret refuge, a first protest against a mother's abandonment.

It is through this subterfuge that the dreamy complexity of the work begins to emerge. The writer, looking as if into a tableau, seeks to remake the former safe haven of her family, though this is no longer a child's game. She understands precisely how foolish the attempt is, yet continues to play because she is on a mission and that is to write a sister back into life.

This she does with growing delight in the first half of the story, marshalling her resources to re-enliven her sister's sassy nature and detail the role she herself played as adoring sidekick: Little Miss Tonto to her sister the Lone Rangeress.

It is not difficult to pinpoint the sources for Frame's writing here, for she is already widely read, a reading much influenced by her mother's taste— Hawthorne, Mark Twain, Dickens, Grimms' fairytales. The sharp schematic quality of American cinema has also worked a cleansing influence on her.

Yet another is surely Katherine Mansfield's New Zealand stories, which also detail a family's life while searching out an authentic indigenous character. With Mansfield, too, she shares a cutting wit that can derail her work, while 'The Secret' itself bears a structural resemblance to Mansfield's 'The Garden Party'.

Frame ventures down psychic corridors closed off to her literary forebear's gamey, rose-lipped intelligence, and, having brought her sister back to life on the page, she proceeds to pitch the reader into something wholly rare and original.

Nini's mother confides in her daughter that her beloved elder sister has a serious illness. She 'may go at any time ... Pass away Nini, be taken by God'.

For her bright, curious, sceptical and shrewdly confident daughter, not yet a teenager, the revelation has disastrous consequences. The first is shock, the second a categorical rejection of the news, then the third, precipitated by this, a loss of faith in her mother's judgement. In rejecting the truth about her sister's condition, Nini loses her anchor in the world and then her bearings altogether. She is utterly bereft, and Frame traces the growing panic that washes into this engaging child's mind with a devastating, clinical accuracy.

Their roles have reversed.

Nini, regarding her mother with exasperated compassion, assumes the responsibility for her sister her mother has reneged on, then goes a step further, taking upon herself the task of mothering her as well.

'My mother looked sad and helpless like the princess in the fairy tale when she has to empty the sea with a thimble ...' (*trimble* in this Caxton edition).

She steps into her shoes and jollies her along. Nini is on top of the problem. She knows about death. It cannot touch her and she describes a number of sadistic experiments undertaken by the sisters that prove her mettle and bear her out: feeding flies to spiders; burning beetles with magnifying glasses.

Here the distances between writer, character and reader begin to close. Nini cannot keep her circling panic at bay, any more than Frame can keep it out of her story. Then we are all in the grip of it.

The mother is baking gingerbread men. They lie in rows on a tray on the kitchen table and begin to come alive as she fixes raisins in for eyes. In just three lines Frame conjures Nini into a Grimm nightmare, through which she attempts to cover her tracks by assuming what she imagines to be the detached reasoning mind of an adult.

She runs through a list of people she knows who have died. They are all elderly and infirm. Concluding that only old people die, she reassures herself, then her mother, about her beloved sister's fate.

'So I smiled to myself when my mother told me the secret, and I put three raisins into my mouth and I said, don't believe the doctor, Mum. It's not true.'

Soon, however, this cocky front begins to unravel. By eating the raisins she has ingested her panic, but she cannot digest it and it re-emerges at night as her world begins to transmute back into the fairytale nightmare. She trips like Hansel and Gretel into a growing horror that is well beyond her ability to manage.

'The shadow of the plum-tree outside was waving up and down on the bedroom wall, and the dark mass of coats at the back of the door made fantastic shapes of troll and dwarf.'

Fuelled by her growing doubt, the panic then settles on her sister, asleep in the same bed, who fails to respond to her call. Nini puts her hand over Myrtle's heart to test it, and 'Lub-dub, lub-dub, lub-dub, her heart was saying'.

So it was all right ...

And here the story ends, with Nini reassured in her judgement, the plum tree once again a plum tree as she settles back in bed and falls to sleep.

But it is not all right, for the story has an after-life that moves the reader, as has been continually threatened, out into the writer's real world. This is a deliberately directed fictional strategy, and how effortlessly up to date it now reads.

Nini's sister is Myrtle, the namesake of Frame's older sister, tragically drowned at seventeen and resurrected here, in character, at sixteen or so, through an act of love. But this love is governed by an implacably chaste honesty. The writer, unlike her character Nini, is not misled about the true nature of Myrtle's fate and uses this knowledge to lard her writing with a deadly irony that entraps the reader.

This can be sensed through a second reading: 'I liked the smell of Myrtle ...' she writes near the beginning of the story. 'She smelt alive.'

This chilling authorial back-hander rises like a spectre from the tale because the writer maintains two opposing views of her character Nini. She is at once a sympathetic, wholly innocent, resourceful girl, and at the same time a hopeless duffer. This realisation is distressing to readers who never quite know where (or how) to hang their sympathy. And what sharpens up that distress is the knowledge that Frame, having drawn a life-line from her sister to the fictionalised character of her sister, can then slide her reader from fiction into real life and back at will. We never quite know which story we are supposed to be in and dither about in puzzlement while the author waits, poised above with metallic curiosity, magnifying glass in hand, for the realisation to dawn that we are as trapped in this tableau as Nini and Myrtle, and Frame and her sister.

There is a Shakespearean quality to this remarkable intellectual adventure that echoes the fierce, melancholic fatalism of Hamlet. Entrapped by what he sees as an implacable fate, he sets about with an arrestingly attractive and wily will to entrap, in turn, not only those he imagines to be his enemies but everyone else in the play, and then the theatre audience, in just this way. He reasons his way forward with a sparklingly frigid determination, while managing in the end simply to inaugurate one more dismal round of savagery.

Because Frame's own pessimism is underpinned by an act of love she reaches out further here than she (or we) can grasp, causing the story's distressing obligation to truth to be continually countermanded by the ambiguity of her language. Here is understanding and confusion, clarity and puzzlement, revelation and concealment, qualities that have been blended together. The understanding confuses, the clarity puzzles, the revelation conceals. Meaning slides around in this exquisitely unbalanced story, in which nothing can ever be quite what it seems.

Here stands literature at its most hallowed; isolated from the world, alone, its sufferings ungovernable, its sense of self unsalvageable, insisting that it protect its identity by acknowledging a helplessness it refuses to bow to, all the while remaining scrupulous in a way that stretches the mind, all the way out to the isolating sanity of a consuming reason.

But writing is not living; mostly it is a distraction from more important business and in the end it stands as a defiant memorial to something and somewhere we may once have been. We are not fixed. Writing cannot fix that, any more than it can bring back the dead or right the wrongs of the past. And there is a trick to it, a sleight of hand that Frame reveals and revels in: to write convincingly you must first understand that you cannot take the world's measure, but in your work you must imagine that you can.

Here is the line she walks: confident and assured in her devastation.

Landfall Review Online

www.landfallreview.com

Reviews posted since October 2017
(reviewer's name in brackets)

October 2017

Family History, Johanna Emeney (Siobhan Harvey)

Night Horse, Elizabeth Smither (Siobhan Harvey)

Wolf, Elizabeth Morton (Claire Mabey)

The Ski Flier, Maria McMillan (Claire Mabey)

Rock & Roll: Selected poems in five sets, Mark Pirie (Liz Breslin)

The Yield, Sue Wootton (Liz Breslin)

A Fugitive Presence, Peter Bland (Liz Breslin)

Astride a Fierce Wind, Huberta Hellendoorn (Redmer Yska)

The Earth Cries Out, Bonnie Etherington (Elizabeth Heritage)

Red Herring, Jonothan Cullinane (Michael Morrissey)

November 2017

Heloise, Mandy Hager (Elizabeth Smither)

Our Future is in the Air, Tim Corballis (Nicholas Reid)

Milk Island, Rhydian Thomas (Jack Ross)

Taking My Jacket for a Walk, Peter Olds (Piet Nieuwland)

The Atomic Composition of Seeming Solids, Shane Hollands (Piet Nieuwland)

Ambient Terror, Victor Billot (Piet Nieuwland)

Black Marks on the White Page, eds Witi Ihimaera & Tina Makereti (Vaughan Rapatahana)

December 2017

Five Strings, Apirana Taylor (Thom Conroy)

RedEdits, Geoff Cochrane (Denis Harold)

Dylan Junkie, Jeffrey Paparoa Holman (Kay McKenzie Cooke)

Waking by a River of Light, John Gibb (Kay McKenzie Cooke)

Alzheimer's and a Spoon, Liz Breslin (Genevieve McLean)

Night Burns with a White Fire: The essential Lauris Edmond, eds Frances Edmond & Sue Fitchett (Genevieve McLean)

Hard Frost: Structures of feeling in New Zealand literature, 1908–1945, John Newton (Nicholas Reid)

Undreamed of … 50 years of the Frances Hodgkins Fellowship, Priscilla Pitts and Andrea Hotere (Andrew Paul Wood)

February 2018

Through the Lonesome Dark, Paddy Richardson (Linda Burgess)

Bad Things, Louise Wallace (Janet Charman)

Kinds of Hunger, Jan Hutchison (Janet Charman)

Ordinary Time, Anna Livesey (Janet Charman)

The Beat of the Pendulum, Catherine Chidgey (Charlotte Grimshaw)

These Two Hands, Renée (Fiona Samuel)

A Strange Beautiful Excitement: Katherine Mansfield's Wellington 1888–1903, Redmer Yska (Helen Watson White)

First Fox, Leanne Radojkovich (Iona Winter)

Waitapu, Helen Margaret Waaka (Iona Winter)

March 2018

Flow, Airini Beautrais (Lynley Edmeades)

Tightrope, Selina Tusitala Marsh (Lynley Edmeades)

Vanishing Points, Michele Leggott (Lynley Edmeades)

White City, David Lyndon Brown (Vaughan Rapatahana)

Forty Years of Titirangi Poets, ed Ron Riddell (Mary Cresswell)

Homeless, John Howell (Mary Cresswell)

⌐Surrender, Janet Charman (Mary Cresswell)

Fletcher of the Bounty, Graeme Lay (Max Oettli)

Johnson, Dean Parker (Michael Morrissey)

Casting Off, Elspeth Sandys (Holly Walker)

The Landfall Review

Moonshine Man: Remembering Russell Haley

by Chris Else

Moonshine Eggs by Russell Haley (Titus Books, 2017), 235pp, $34

I first met Russell Haley in 1966, a short while after he and his family moved to New Zealand. I was then in my second year at Auckland Teachers' College and Russell's wife Jean was in her first year. I can't remember how our meeting came about but it seems, in retrospect, to have been inevitable. Russell and Jean and their two children were living in Morgan Street in Newmarket. My first memories of him are of sitting in one of their front rooms, which he used as a study, and raving about writing.

Russell did most of the talking. He was a typical extravert; he drew creative strength from sharing what he was working on. I am just as typical an introvert; I get worried that saying too much too soon will destroy the magic. We differed in other ways, too. I was writing short stories and the beginnings of novels that always failed to get beyond 10,000 words, working in a variety of styles and genres in a haphazard search for a literary direction. Russell was writing plays with the confidence of someone who knew exactly what he was doing.

They weren't the kind of plays I was used to back then. They weren't realistic or classically formed; they didn't have conventional plots; they weren't focussed on the psychological examination of particular characters. Instead, they were surrealistic explorations of ideas drawn from Russell's eclectic reading. They bristled with energy, wit and joy at the possibilities of language, an exuberance that transcended and redeemed any dark tendencies in the subject matter.

I owe a big debt to those conversations. At the time, I was occasionally resentful that our almost exclusive focus on *his* work meant I was doing all the giving and he the receiving. In fact, I was learning heaps— far more than he was—and when I did finally find a direction for my work I was guided by my own take on the playfulness and irony that Russell was so good at.

By the late sixties Russell's interests had shifted to poetry. He became a leading member of the movement that centred round the magazine *Freed*. Along with the likes of Alan Brunton, Mark Young and David Mitchell, Haley mounted a challenge to the poetical forms and practice of the preceding decades. For the *Freed* writers, who also called themselves the Cultural Liberation Front, poetry was not carefully considered words on a page but performance, an in your face and out there protest that matched the anti-war and anti-apartheid marches on the streets.

In his introduction to *The Big Smoke* (AUP, 2000), an anthology that celebrates the New Zealand poetry of the sixties and early seventies, of which *Freed* was a notable part, Alan Brunton describes the temper of the times as paranoid: the sense that reality is out to get you. Haley's work has often reflected this. It contrasts with the literary mode of the previous generation—the prose of Frank Sargeson and A.P. Gaskell, for example—which is characterised by a psychic distance, a cool detachment that, in its turn, might derive from a sense of alienation: the source of the search for that phantasm 'a national identity'. In Haley there is no such separation; reality intrudes; it traps you; it has to be confronted and dealt with no matter how difficult or bizarre it turns out to be. The title of his second book of short stories, *Real Illusions* (VUP, 1984), reflects this engagement: in the writer's mind there is no distinction between fact and invention. In the story *Occam's Electric Razor*, for example, the protagonist, Holliday, cleans a razor that once belonged to his deceased father and dislodges a block of shaven hair that mirrors, in its chromatic layers, the aging of his father's beard. Holliday goes on to shave his father's cowhide slippers to produce black leather moulds of the dead man's feet and thereby conjures up his father's ghost. Use of autobiographical detail is a hallmark of Haley's work and my guess, from the precision of the description, is that the razor and the block of hair were real and, maybe, the slippers too; inherited as the story suggests, in a box of stuff from Haley's own father. The concrete detail provides a launching pad for the surrealist flight to the story's conclusion. *Occam's Electric Razor* encapsulates a major

preoccupation: the idea that each of us creates our own reality but our created worlds are never under our control.

From the mid-eighties Haley began to explore longer fictional forms. He continued to work on short stories but they often occurred in sequences, such as *The Transfer Station* (Nagare Press, 1989). There were also a number of novels. Gradually, too, the surrealism became naturalised to the point where in *The Spaces Between* (Adastra Productions, 2012) the questions that torment the protagonist might all be interpreted as symptoms of the injuries he has suffered when attacked by unknown assailants, rather than as threats from the offbeat medical institution he finds himself in.

In 2000 Hazard Press republished *The Transfer Station* along with another sequence of stories, *A Spider-Web Season*. This latter work introduced Haley's most endearing creation: Harry Rejekt, whose name has genuine provenance beyond its obvious connotation. Harry appeared a second time in *Tomorrow Tastes Better* (HarperCollins, 2001). *Moonshine Eggs* is his third and last appearance; Haley died of a brain tumour in 2016.

Harry is a middle-aged bachelor who lives with his border collie-cross, Sako, in a crumbling cottage overlooking Lake Karapiro. He is eccentric, romantic and self-sufficient. He is looking for love but is beset by doubt and diffidence, which make engaging with women a delicate and difficult business with a high risk of failure. *Moonshine Eggs* sees him still working for the fat and worldly Joseph Bartleby in a Tirau second-hand shop and yearning for a reunion with Shelly Nairn, whom he met briefly in Thames in the second book.

In his introduction to *Moonshine Eggs*, Murray Edmond explores the theme of poetry threaded through the novel and the way it reflects Haley himself:

> To an extent, [Harry] is Russell's self-imagining. His initials, HR, are a deliberate inversion of Russell Haley's own, RH. So, Harry is also the reverse of his author. Whereas Harry dreams of being a poet, Russell was a poet. Before he was a poet, he was a dramatist. And after he was a poet, he was a fiction writer. The character of Harry emerges from this lineage ... as the embodiment of Russell Haley's mature work, a comical, insightful, puzzled, tentative, curious, insignificant, imaginative being whose whimsicality is oddly grounded by an improbable sanity. (p.8)

The key word here is 'embodiment'. Edmond suggests that Harry is not only a reflection of his creator but also has a reflexive relationship to Haley's other work. This second relationship arises from the dynamic interplay in Haley's use of his own fact and fiction.

Harry is an odd mixture of passivity and spontaneity. Whenever he is faced with a self-initiated decision, such as making a trip to Tasmania to finally connect with Shelly, he talks himself out of it or lapses into inertia; but if a problem or a new situation presents itself—whether it be a wardrobe that turns out to be full of borer, a length of broken guttering on the cottage, or a wandering Japanese student who has no money and nowhere to sleep—he responds with decision, creativity,

practical skill and generosity. His character is essentially reactive; it thrives on what life throws at it. This is the interface in which the earlier stories operate and for which paranoia is the metaphor. In Harry, paranoia emerges as a constant anxiety about how he appears to other people, a concern that finds a marvellous solution in a typical Rejekt invention:

> ... you never actually knew how you looked, did you, when you weren't staring into a shaving mirror? You had a vague idea of course. Your facial muscles moved when you smiled. But could you feel what you looked like when you were pissed off, sarcastic, randy? Perhaps actors could but they weren't like ordinary people ... As an ordinary human being you looked out at the world through a spotless window and if you squinted and focussed hard you could just see the surface of the glass. What you really needed, though, for ... feedback, that was the word, what was required was a kind of offset mirror device so that you could read your own expression and look beyond to the other person. You could call it a selfoscope. One of those neck braces, some stainless steel rods, and an adapted rear-vision mirror would do the trick. If anyone in the street asked you why you were wearing this contraption you could say you don't know where you're going if you don't know where you are from. You have to keep your head immobilised because you've broken your neck. You fell while looking at a rainbow. (pp.144–45)

Harry exemplifies the creative spirit of ordinary people, a man-alone figure who is yet fully connected with the life around him: funny, wise and capable and, like his creator, one of the kindest men you could ever wish to meet.

Shaken into View

by Stephanie Johnson

Decline and Fall on Savage Street by Fiona Farrell (Vintage, 2017), 360pp, $38

'Our homes are a protective shell and when that shell cracks, we are born into another kind of being. It is not just glass and masonry that require repair but our whole sense of who we are. It is not just the structure of the home that is shaken into view, but the entire structure within which we live our lives.' So writes Fiona Farrell towards the end of *The Villa at the Edge of the Empire*, the companion book to *Decline and Fall on Savage Street*. The companion is the older book, published in 2015, while *Decline and Fall* appeared last year. Both take as their subject the devastation of Christchurch after the earthquakes, the first as a work of non-fiction and the second as a novel.

If the books are read one after the other, as this reviewer did, one could expect, in the hands of a lesser writer, a certain weariness of the subject. Even at the time of the earthquakes there was a polarity of attitude to discussions about them—many New Zealanders rapidly grew tired of hearing about it, while Christchurch justifiably felt abandoned. Those of us who know the city, especially those who have lived there for periods of our lives or who continue to do so, can only regard Farrell's twin publications as precious taonga.

Fiona Farrell is a marvellously inventive writer, as demonstrated by much of her earlier work. *Book Book* is a lively and entertaining mix of memoir and fiction, inspired by a life's experience of reading; *The Hopeful Traveller* can be read from either end. Likewise, *Decline and Fall on Savage Street* should not be approached as a conventional novel. Farrell takes as her central idea a house on Savage Street in the Avon Loop, an old part of the city that was badly affected by the shaking and liquefaction. The novel is a biography of the house, beginning in 1906 before the suburb has been built, and ending mid-2012 with heart-breaking demolition. There is a scope, therefore, of over a hundred years. American Jane Smiley attempts similar coverage in her *The Last Hundred Years*, but spreads it out over three rather stodgy, heavy-going volumes detailing the fortunes of a mid-Western farming family.

Decline and Fall is far from stodgy. It races along at a rapid pace, introducing a plethora of characters. Some of the inhabitants are only briefly resident, just as they would be in life; others live at the address for years, and so reappear in consecutive chapters. As if it were a house itself, the book depends heavily on its architectural design. Chapters are headed with a year and month, and it is usually spring. Each begins with an ellipsis so that the reader is plunged straight into the story of the next occupants. This is at times irksome, although it has the effect of lulling the reader into the idea of a continuum: that we enter the lives of the characters and then depart again with the sense that we have been treated to a snapshot of their day-to-day life.

Further to its design, the book is divided into two parts, the first detailing the years until 2010. After that the narration is slower and more considered, and gives the reader time to engage with the characters and their dilemmas. Interspersed between the chapters are short pieces concerning a female eel that lives in the Avon River near the house. She has her own very short chapters in which she hangs in the murky water, growing ever larger and avoiding capture before eventually setting off on her migration north, as all eels do.

In the companion book, Farrell gives us the Māori history of the greater area before the arrival of Europeans, but here she contents herself with the Pākehā intention for this smaller zone. In 1906 Savage Street is a sand dune with surveyors' pegs marking out future sections. By 1908 the house is a drawing, and by 1910 the builders are at work. The house is a fine example of its period, with verandahs, an inglenook, a turret and coloured glass panes in the front door. By 1912 there are children living at the address, playing in the river and having adventures. One of these is a girl called Sibyl, who will live in the house all her life. She is an artist with an antipathy to housework, and the house crumbles around her. Surrounded by cats, dogs and vermin, she lets out rooms to tenants

and cares for her ailing elderly mother, whom we have known since her youth in earlier chapters. After Sibyl's death the house is derelict and abandoned. In 1970 some alternative life-stylers use it as a commune. Through the eighties and until the earthquakes, various families of ascending social scale live there. The reader is acquainted with all of them, some intimately—just as one would be with neighbours who live next door for years—and others only glancingly, since they move on quickly. This is at times frustrating, and there is also the occasional impression that Farrell is struggling to insert enough backstory into these narratives to give the characters meaning. If the reader approaches the book as a series of interlinked short stories, it is a more satisfying read.

The wider world is present. Sons are lost in the Great War; the Depression bites hard; Jewish refugees arrive from Europe ahead of World War II. Industrial unrest stirs the early 1950s. There is the Queen's visit in the early fifties and the Beatles in 1964; in 1968 Luka the space dog glides overhead; in 1972 a hippy is compelled to go to Australia for an abortion as it's still difficult to get hold of the Pill. In the eighties there are protests, in the nineties computers arrive and a blended family with professional jobs bemoans cuts to health and education.

Always, the language is light and inventive. There are flashes of humour and thunderbolts of anger, particularly in the second part. Not only does Farrell express outrage against the bumbling of the earthquake assessors, mostly inept and inexperienced Australians, there is also fury with The Buffoon, an unnamed Gerald Brownlee, and his destruction of many heritage buildings that could have been preserved. The desecration is further afield than the city—a character in the second half is alarmed and dismayed by the intensification of dairy farming on the Canterbury Plains and the consequent ruination of rivers and streams. In February 2011, just before the second big quake, he thinks of the herds of dairy cows:

> Those poor bloody creatures you saw everywhere now, moping on big bare paddocks, wagging the stumps of their amputated tails ... Just big pink sacs really, on their skinny legs, squeezing out milk powder for Chinese baby formula, Chinese ice cream, Chinese dietary supplements. And hadn't he read somewhere that the Chinese were allergic to lactose?

Fiona Farrell was herself a long-time resident of Canterbury. Her depiction of the eerie fountains of liquefaction rising in what were previously well-kept grounds of the Garden City, and of the intense distress suffered, particularly by children, is deeply affecting. I will not be the only reader to finish *Decline and Fall on Savage Street* with teary eyes. The book is a work of great maturity, wisdom and insight. It is nothing less than a scandal that it was ignored by the Ockham Book Prize—further proof that the prize is becoming increasingly irrelevant.

On the Road and on the Run
by Owen Marshall

Tess by Kirsten McDougall (Victoria University Press, 2017), 156pp, $25

This is Kirsten McDougall's second book of fiction and her first novel. It is a short work, but that is no bad thing because it is direct, pacey and intense, with central characters of interest and issues concerning which the author has strong feelings.

The story opens with 19-year-old Tess on the road and on the run from a violent and undisclosed past. She is befriended by 45-year-old Lewis, who, it turns out, is also fleeing his past, but in a psychological sense. Sick and traumatised, Tess accepts Lewis's invitation to stay a while in his Masterton home and a tentative friendship develops, despite their very different backgrounds and ages. Lewis is a dentist and well established; Tess's mother was a drug addict, and Tess's childhood was less than ideal and her schooling incomplete. She was brought up by her grandmother Sheila, with whom she shares the ability to see at times into the lives of others and access their most vivid memories. Tess has found this as much a burden as a gift, and the supernatural element is downplayed, successfully integrated into the pervasive realism of the story rather than dramatised.

McDougall wisely avoids the obvious plot line of a sexual relationship between Tess and Lewis, instead developing a subtle and interesting bond of friendship and mutual support. Lewis's wife was killed in tragic circumstances, which resulted in alienation from his twin son and daughter—Jonti and Jean. Through Tess, a certain amount of family reconciliation is achieved towards the conclusion of the novel, but any happy ending is thwarted by the sudden intrusion of Tess's former partner, and the novel concludes as it began—Tess alone, on the road, running away.

McDougall is a serious writer in the best sense, wishing her story and characters to lead readers to a consideration of their own lives and the society around them. There are themes of friendship and love, of the complexity and importance of family support and relationships, of isolation and self worth, and of the vulnerability that many women feel in today's society and the type of men who are the cause of that apprehension.

The structure of the novel is well designed and successful: a series of short chapters with even shorter sections within them, and a progressive revelation of the characters' back stories that maintains suspense. Sentences too tend to linear compactness. No meandering asides, no drawn out descriptions of local colour, although the setting is established succinctly and with power. McDougall is an observant writer with an eye for telling detail, for idiosyncrasy,

and she has a talent for pithy, original images that glint within the text:

> Neat grids of paddocks stretched out either side of them, their boundaries lined with tidy rows of eucalypts and macrocarpas, wire fences beneath them. Sheep and cows dotted the grass like a scattershot of ornaments. He felt the pleasure of the green wash over his eyes.

> All she could see was some sort of shifting emotion in Lewis's face, like a cloud making shapes over a landscape, as he tried to understand what she was telling him.

> She moved further into the water until she was up to her thighs. The cold felt like a pure metal and she could feel her skin numbing. The water shone under the bright sun and the world was all surfaces and senses—the rough cry of cicadas, the rushing sound of the trees, the glittering light on the leaves, the fire of the sun radiating off the rocks and the icy river.

McDougall is especially assured when describing bodily physical experiences: Tess's sickness for example, which is the initial reason for her stay in Lewis's home.

> She touched her lower back and felt that her T-shirt was wet through. Her hair stuck to her neck with sweat. She quickly pulled the T-shirt over her head and undid her bra and threw them both on the ground. She lifted her hair up in a bunch and let the cool air calm the skin around her throat and neck. Her body felt hollow and achy. It's bad, she thought, and knew now it had been coming on for a day or two.

She is less sure with dialogue. A couple uses each other's name repeatedly in conversation, which is not usual in everyday life. Sometimes the young people's Kiwi idioms and obscenities seem rather forced, and at other times the conversation of middle-aged Lewis and Alan, the doctor, seems slightly stilted, as if the author is consciously striving to differentiate the language of the generations.

> Jean, all I've ever wanted is for my children to be happy. That's been very hard to achieve, much harder than I thought. But in the last week I've seen you happier than you've been since you were a little girl. I see the effect that Tess has had on you, on our household, and I'm very grateful.

The opening of the novel is particularly strong and intriguing and claims the reader's attention, and the development of the relationship between Tess and Lewis is equally absorbing. About half way through the story Jean and Jonti are introduced as significant players. This increases the scope of the story, and a further thematic element is introduced when Tess and Jean fall in love. No doubt it is intended as an enrichment of both cast and concerns, but the result is a noticeable swerve in the novel's direction. The love between the two young women is handled well enough, despite seeming to have a somewhat abrupt beginning after considerable antagonism between the two, but the focus of the novel shifts and the relationship between Tess and Lewis, which I found the more interesting, unusual and multi-layered, is somewhat sidelined.

In comparison with the apparently effortless accomplishment of much that goes before, the ending also suffers to a degree. Tess's ex-boyfriend, the violent Benny, one of the more stereotypical figures, turns up on new year's eve with an equally Clockwork Orange sidekick, and there is a contrived and violent climax in which Benny gets shot. For some stories and some writers, a fireworks display of dramatic action is necessary to compensate for deficiencies in more subtle aspects of the fiction. Neither McDougall nor her story need recourse to that, and it's a pity she didn't trust to her readers in this regard and have a more muted yet satisfying and natural end. She is at her impressive best when not obviously striving for heightened impact and surprise.

Overall, however, this is a novel that has reason for existence and is thought-provoking and enjoyable. McDougall has heartfelt things to say and admirable language skills with which to express them. The themes are apposite and contemporary, the voice strong and original. The novel is well served, too, by its eye-catching cover.

Coercion
by Chris Tse

What Is Left Behind by Tom Weston (Steele
Roberts, 2017), 76pp, $25; **Rumpelstiltskin
Blues** by John Adams (Steele Roberts, 2017)
88pp, $25; **Tales of the Waihorotiu** by Carin
Smeaton (Titus Books, 2017) 88pp, $25

In a recent radio interview, Napier-based
poet David Chan was asked whether his
day job as a lawyer infiltrated his creative
life. Although Chan said he preferred to
keep the two separate, he did muse on
the similarity between the legal
profession and poetry, describing law as
'coercion translated into language'. He
went on to say that writing poetry is, in a
sense, coercion—a poet's aim should be
to coerce the reader into a new way of
thinking by using language to pull back
the curtains on other lives. In doing so,
they can challenge perceptions and
perhaps even change ways of thinking.

Three recent poetry collections each
use language in dynamic ways to push
the reader into states of reflection and
revelation—two of them also happen to
be written by former judges. These three
books perform acts of linguistic coercion
that lead the reader into very different
worlds.

An enduring absence permeates Tom
Weston's *What Is Left Behind*, a collection
that drifts quietly over scenes of broken
cities and fading moments. Weston, a
barrister and former judge, uses his

carefully constructed poems to examine
the effects of loss and time, giving equal
weight to what remains and what has
been taken. In the title poem, Weston
writes:

> You reach for what is left.
> And, sometimes, the spaces are filled again.
> …
>
> A thing lost in the periphery of now is lost for
> all time.

Throughout the collection people are
constantly searching for ways to retrieve
or return to the past: photographs,
indentations in fabric, anecdotes and
rituals all play a part in reaching for what
was once there. In Weston's book the
past is always something to look back at,
not to fulfil that human need for
nostalgia but to make sense of the
present and perhaps the future. How
then to navigate and collapse those
distances, both physical and temporal,
that keep the present tethered to the
past?

The use of fire as a recurring image
emphasises Weston's preoccupation with
memorialising what has been lost. The
fires in this book are both destructive and
cleansing, and fire itself can be
consumed by fire.

One of the most visceral
manifestations of absence and loss is
grief. The fantastic long sequence
'Crossing over' is a meditation on how
grief can settle in our lives, entrenching
its 'many voices' in the tiny folds of the
everyday until it is 'in retreat but /
disputing those who claimed the day'.
This poem is an excellent example of

Weston's technical abilities and the emotional balance that informs much of his work, where the intellectual examination of his chosen themes is offset by recognisable human responses.

A development in contemporary video games is the shift to 'fourth-person' games, whereby a player has no control over a main character. Instead, the player manipulates aspects of the environment to influence the central character's decisions. This indirect control of the character is similar to what it's like to be a reader in Weston's poetic world. Weston's assured hand is felt but remains just out of sight. There is a lightness to the way he presents a scene or introduces a specific detail, guiding our attention without overtly controlling whatever meaning we might take from one of his poems.

Reviewers of Weston's previous collections have made mention of his penchant for the abstract.

Many of the poems in this collection demand careful reading (in some cases, re-reading) in order to fully appreciate the sheer scope of each individual poem. It would, of course, be careless to suggest that such poetry is 'hard work' or difficult to 'get'. There is abstraction at play in Weston's poems, but its overall effect is to create a sense of emotional immersion, rather than manipulating language to confuse or disguise meaning. On the contrary, Weston's use of language is crisp and tight without feeling overworked or calculated, lending his poems a certain poise and stability.

Perhaps Weston says it best himself in 'Landscape without boat':

> The master was careful in his choice of
>   words,
>
> aware that definition
> could not be ignored—or no longer
>
> and not so easily.

Weston is a poet of great intelligence and insight—this is a collection to savour and take your time with.

In *Rumpelstiltskin Blues*, John Adams takes the well-known fairy tale character and uses him as an avatar of sorts in poems that move briskly through themes of family, memory and regret. It's a fulsome book, squeezing 73 poems into its 88 pages, and although some of the poems don't quite earn their inclusion, there is plenty of gold to be found.

The story of Rumpelstiltskin is riddled with morally bankrupt men who exploit a young woman for professional and personal gain. This is a fairy tale that involves lies getting out of hand, a hostage situation and human trafficking. Curious, then, that Adams has chosen Rumpelstiltskin to represent his own role as a poet, one who takes the straw of life and spins it into literary gold.

The book's blurb asks, 'Who is Rumpelstiltskin? … Evil or misunderstood? Would a good lawyer have helped?' These questions of truth and morality echo some that were asked in Adams' previous collection *Briefcase*, a novella in verse that told the story of a domestic violence incident through legal documents. Where *Briefcase* was an experimental work of fiction inspired by his dealings as a judge, *Rumpelstiltskin Blues* is the flipside: a markedly more personal collection that turns the lens on Adams himself and those around him. There are many wonderful poems about—and dedicated to—family and friends.

Threads of Adams' past are woven throughout this book, as if Adams is taking stock of his life, picking over formative memories and events that he hasn't been able to let go. This is set up very effectively in the opening poem, which recalls his time as a District and Family Court judge:

> Five years I've been turned
> over; disturbed
>
> by my reflections.
> I've taken many a baby
>
> from its mummy.

Much like the way Weston's legal background manifests itself as he experiments with language and meaning, Adams uses his own experiences in law as a means to embellish his chosen themes, resulting in wordplay that employs double meanings to draw parallels between his public and private lives. In Adams' world, a poem is a crime scene—'we must bring all data to trial', he writes in 'Trial by poetry'—but is it his role or the reader's to carry out the forensic examination?

The questions that propel this collection prompt the reader to weigh in on Adams' own self-reflection on what it

means to have had a profound effect on others' lives, and how one might be judged by one's own actions. By using Rumpelstiltskin as a stand-in, Adams finds himself navigating the grey areas of life—the murky in-between where there are no easy answers or free passes, regardless of the positions of power one might hold.

As much as the collection is about reflecting on the past, it also acknowledges the need to draw a line in the sand and move forward. In 'Docking out', a poem that marks his retirement as a judge, Adams says it's 'time to adopt / a new position'. For a collection that spends most of its time soul-searching for answers, the one Adams settles on is somewhat sobering, as it accepts he will eventually be considered archaic and obsolete: 'After a decent / lapse, / I should sink / out of reference.'

The Waihorotiu in the title of Carin Smeaton's first book, *Tales of the Waihorotiu*, is a stream that flows beneath Queen Street in Auckland's CBD, long since covered up by the progress of urbanisation. It's an apt image that lends itself to being a metaphorical backbone of sorts for the collection. An undercurrent of dissatisfaction and unease flows beneath these poems, which give voice to those who struggle to live in a city that has either forgotten them or is increasingly pushing them to the fringes. But Smeaton hasn't forgotten them, and in this collection she shares their stories of struggle and survival.

These poems are confronting, but necessarily so.

Smeaton has a commanding voice in telling it like it is, peeling back the shiny packaging to expose what's broken with contemporary society. The world is a divided place—this division plays out in comments sections, on social media, and in the verbal sparring of politicians who insist they know what's best for us. Smeaton is not concerned with glamorising that division or using it to make it a point. Instead, her poems are presented as snapshots that place the people front and centre—the family, friends and strangers that make up this collection are what really matter. They drift through this book, passing each other like characters in a Robert Altman ensemble, playing out their lives in modern-day Auckland. Whether it's a 'disarming soprano guy' she watches shuffle off the bus, or the bus driver who swears 'real low at the lights / missing an orange by a whisker', Smeaton plants just enough detail for us to both get a sense of these people and to create our own backstories for them—as she does herself throughout the collection.

Where Weston and Adams' use of language is arguably more polished, Smeaton uses slang and Kiwi vernacular to create a casual and often gossip-like tone to pull the reader closer into the worlds she has granted us access to. At times it feels like a friend telling you a story that they heard from so-and-so, who heard from so-and-so, and so on. Does this dilute the content of the poems? Not at all. Through Smeaton, we have become the latest recipients in this chain of whispers. This intimacy is emphasised by her use of short, punchy lines and the absence of punctuation marks:

> the goss used to be worth da read
> on dem steps
> on the way up to the flying fox
> anyway
> there'd always be talk
> & people do talk
> says jo

Although this can be jarring to begin with, it has the dual effect of demanding your attention as a reader, forcing you to pause and consider each phrase or image. Smeaton isn't concerned with being 'proper', and her poetry is all the better for it.

The collection closes with a series of ten longer, almost prose-like poems that I found the most compelling. These extended pieces show off Smeaton's strength in creating and sustaining different voices, and as character studies they feel much more vivid than the shorter snapshots in the poems that came before.

Tales of the Waihorotiu is a welcome debut and introduces a distinct voice in contemporary New Zealand poetry.

Deeply Divided
by Ray Grover

Phoney Wars: New Zealand society in the Second World War by Stevan Eldred-Grigg with Hugh Eldred-Grigg (Otago University Press, 2017), 427pp, $49.95

Phoney Wars is a beautifully produced book. In it Stevan and Hugh Eldred-Grigg maintain that New Zealand should not have fought World War II as it did, and that the reality of war was never really known on the home front except by those who suffered the loss of close relatives serving overseas. While there is evidence for the latter claim, the substantiation they give for the former is questionable—as it is for a number of other issues they raise.

The authors believe that the Vietnam War was in some ways not unlike the war against Nazi Germany. In each case, they say, a powerful ally (Britain in 1939 and America in 1964) bullied New Zealand to fight their ideological enemy. They seek to demonstrate that Fraser's government sacrificed far more than it needed to, while the Holyoake government was adept enough to give America no more than the basic minimum required to maintain the defence connection. This likening of the two wars startles with its superficiality. World War II—which the authors describe as 'short'—was above all else a war of foreign conquest and resistance to it. It was the largest in history, fought in Asia, Africa, Europe and the oceans of the world with more than 40 million combatants and 55 million deaths. The Vietnam War, although also horrific and profoundly exacerbated by American intervention, was essentially a civil war that cost two million Vietnamese their lives along with 58,000 Americans plus some of their very few allies. Thousands of New Zealanders—and thousands of Americans, Australians and other nations—demonstrated against it. Our ties with the US—apart from Anzus—were miniscule compared with those to Britain in the 1930s. Moreover, after our casualty rates in World Wars I and II (when more of our soldiers were killed per head of population than those of any other English-speaking ally), our taste for overseas wars was becoming somewhat satiated.

'The war,' we are told, 'contrary to the propaganda of the time and to subsequent memory, did not unite New Zealanders, it divided them.' In their attempts to validate this and other assertions, the authors tend to edit their sources to fit their preconceptions. For example, in 1940 '[b]ranches [of the Peace and Anti-Conscription Council] were formed throughout the country and crowds kept gathering; a throng of perhaps 6000 … flocked one night to a street meeting in Wellington.' This is derived from an *Evening Post* report, the gist being:

> PACIFIST MEETING, SPEAKERS REMOVED BY POLICE, A GOOD HUMOURED CROWD … A large crowd between 5000 and 6000 … The Mayor attempted to speak, but because of interruptions and general noise … could not be heard more than a few feet away … For the

most part the crowd were good humoured, but individual arguments took place … and some of them led to scuffles that were broken up by the crowd. When pacifist speakers arrived a group of soldiers … who had been filling in the time with an impromptu community sing, shouted out: 'Here comes Hitler' and other comments which caused general laughter. Large numbers of returned soldiers were scattered throughout the gathering. The crowd remained … until nearly 10 p.m. when they melted away, having evidently decided that entertainment was at an end …

In their claim that New Zealand was deeply divided during the war the authors fail to recognise that there was nothing like the anti-Vietnam marches, let alone the Depression riots. Among working-class people there would have been an undercurrent of anti-war feeling but the book has no in-depth analysis of it. Some unions were against the war but how much direct action did they take? Left-wing Labour was also against, but how many were there? 'Citizens of Irish, German, Scandinavian and Croatian ancestry were not likely to see themselves as kith, let alone kin to the British' is another claim. Quite so, but the evidence does not indicate that many were uncooperative enough to be detained—although German-born citizens were.

'Māori were divided in their opinions about the British Empire.' That is so, and I remember being told by a Māori boy that if the Japanese landed, they would kill Pākehā but not Māori. The authors then state that 'Rātana was by far the most widely followed faith among the Māori and many of its faith felt warmly towards Japan.' Maybe many Rātana did, except that even by 1956 they were still third after

Anglican and Catholic Māori. And, out of a total population of fewer than 100,000, almost 16,000 Māori volunteered for war service.

The authors go on to say that when US Marines landed in New Zealand, Māori found 'the racism so common among American troops … shocking'. They may well have, but that may have depended on which Māori and where they happened to be. *Some Modern Maoris* (NZCER, 1946), a sociological survey by Earnest and Pearl Beaglehole, states:

> The Maoris found the marines easy to get on with, very much easier in fact than pakeha New Zealanders. The marines had fine manners said one; another remarked on their ready generosity; a third considered them sympathetic because 'they were all homesick and therefore made us think of our boys homesick in foreign lands'; a fourth decided after talking to some marines that she and they had common attitudes to the Negroes—'a very poor race, I can't stand the look of them …'

Then there is a letter to our first Secretary of Foreign Affairs from Cairo, 13 December 1946, written by D.P. Costello, quoted on pp. 229–30 of Malcolm Templeton's *Ties of Blood and Empire* (AUP, 1994):

> … the Maoris tend to think of themselves not as ordinary coloured people but as something special (just as we are not *white* but pakeha, God bless the mark) which would naturally weaken their solidarity with other species of darkies (I have myself heard Maori soldiers in Egypt address the natives of the country as 'f-cking wogs)—

The latter insult was used by the majority of New Zealand's soldiers, whom the authors rightly take to task on the matter.

Then there were the pacifists and other active war-resisters sent to prison camps and jail. As quoted, the religious historian P.J. Linehan states, 'Conscientious objectors were not thin on the ground, however, indeed they were more common in New Zealand than in most other countries ...' Unquoted, however, is what he says next: 'Nevertheless, support for the war from Catholics, Maori and industrial workers was much more than it had been during the First World War ...', and further on, 'the war brought the New Zealand community together, and any study of emergent nationalism must treat it of great significance'. The total number of activists interned reached 600—out of a population of 1.7 million. (As the authors mention, this imprisonment was, to our shame, the highest per head of population of the English-speaking allies.)

New Zealand's ties to Britain are heavily downplayed. Regarding trade, the authors claim our exports were not quite as critical as the politicians believed, despite stating that 70 per cent of our export earnings came from Britain. Actually, in the 1930s, it was over 80 per cent and we had one of the highest foreign trade ratios per capita in the world. They rail at this but, as we were to learn in the 1970s, it takes time to modify overseas trade. They also appear to have little understanding that, apart from gold, all metals and most products made of them had to be imported, as did petrol, paper, rubber, sugar, and all textiles apart from wool.

Testimony abounds that the deep social, cultural and historical ties were not, as the authors claim, largely confined to the Anglo/Scots upper crust. For example, Kevin Ireland in his account of his left-wing working-class childhood, *Under the Bridge and Over the Moon* (Vintage, 1998) says: '... our attention was almost totally focussed on ... Britain—which everyone referred to as "home" or the "mother country"'. Another, slightly up the social scale, is Bryan Gould's *Goodbye to All That* (Macmillan, 1995): 'New Zealand was the centre of the universe. We were dimly aware that there was a wider world out there somewhere, but the only bits that concerned us ... were Britain (which loomed large as mother country and major trading partner) ... the United States ... and Australia ...'

If any further evidence is needed of the strength of New Zealand's British ties in the 1930s, one only has to look at the situation 80 years later when, despite Britain's demonstrated incapacity to provide defence during World War II and its ditching of us for the Common Market (ha ha), we declined to get rid of the Union Jack and continue to have a British monarch as our head of state.

John McLeod's *Myth and Reality: The New Zealand soldier in World War II* (Reed, 1986) is still the only debunking of war mythology in which we might have confidence. Parts of *Phoney Wars* are substantiated, but there are too few of them.

Astonishing Objects, Hoarded and Polished

by Genevieve Scanlan

Hoard by Fleur Adcock (Victoria University Press, 2017), 96pp, $25; **Field Notes** by Mary Cresswell (Mākaro Press, 2017), 68pp, $25; **Luminescent** by Nina Powles (Seraph Press, 2017), five 20-page chapbooks, $25

Fleur Adcock's striking new collection *Hoard* is aptly named—and not only because it consists of poems held back from other collections. The poems themselves are littered with a hoard of objects: coins, typewriters, green towels … the detritus of a life, all of it signifying something. The writerly impulse to collect is signposted early on in 'The anaesthetist', which sees Adcock invited to view a Caesarean: 'I hardly knew him; / but grist: yes, he saw I collected that.'

In four sections, these poems address histories both political and personal— sometimes questioning their own impulse to reveal. 'Surely you can't like knowing that?' the poet asks, having detailed an ancestor's luckless marriage. But of course, we do—and no wonder. These poems are sharp, at times self-deprecating, wry and darkly humorous. Yet there are also bursts of stunning lyricism; Adcock is as clear-eyed about beauty as she is about pain. 'A spinney' is a love-letter to English trees: 'But the adults never understood it: / our co-

conspirator at the wood's edge, / climbable, flowering or knobbly with dolls' fruit.'

Adcock has a full life's worth of grist to sift through, and a consciousness of this permeates the collection. 'Hot baths' begins, 'These days when anxious friends confide in me / about their intimate medical problems / it's never that they're afraid they're pregnant.'

It's clear that Adcock doesn't mourn the loss of the perils that come with youth: 'Hot baths' reflects that the old wives' remedy for unwanted pregnancy only leaves you unhappily drunk— 'sickening, really'. Like many of these poems, it transmutes harsh experience into something useful. 'Bender' makes vivid the disconcerting effects of distorted eyesight, while framing warped perspective as a talent, an Uri Geller-style trick. Several poems deal with Adcock's marriage to Barry Crump, and this too becomes grist: 'But enough of that (although yes, I won).'

Several poems express anxieties about changing landscapes, both social and physical. In 'Fowlds Park' the poet laments: 'The bastards will get their hands on it—sure to; / they will come with their development schemes'. And though I'd sworn that if I ever read another poem about smartphones it would be too soon, 'Pacifiers' is one I'll concede has a point. Adcock's wit is too wry, her perspective too nuanced to join in the millenial-bashing of thinkpieces everywhere. Instead, she quietly points to similarity within difference: 'They clutch at their phones the way we used to reach for / a packet of Silk Cut: separation anxiety, a blocky shape to fondle in your pocket.'

The final section takes the reader on a kind of road trip around New Zealand, and—perhaps unsurprisingly—in these poems ironic detachment and affection intermingle. From 'Ruakaka' to 'Tinakori Road', the ghostly presence of literary giants is felt: 'How they haunted us! KM and Iris, / Elizabeth Percy in Alnwick castle, / and Eleanor; Eleanor.' The collection's last poem, 'Lotus land', is gorgeous and somehow relenting, looking on the country with a softer eye: 'Walk along Willis Street or Lambton Quay / and you can buy cherries at roadside stalls, / shipped up from the South Island for Christmas ...'

A title like Field Notes might seem to suggest a sober scientific treatise, but Mary Cresswell's latest collection is a frolic—through literal fields, and the field of literature. There is an unabashed delight in these poems: delight in poetic form, in literary allusion, in language's capacity to find beauty in the quotidian.

Linguistic play is presented as a natural impulse early on in 'Landscape with hopelessly restless figures': 'In the car they whined and they squabbled: / limericks, word games for hours, forever.' But for Cresswell, word games are not a last resort, a mere distraction; they are her modus operandi. These are ostentatiously poetical poems, ranging widely in form and revelling in rhyme. Literary allusions abound, from the more oblique—like the familiar cadence of 'a band / a host of silver spinifex'—to the overtly signposted. 'Evoking the muse (2)' begins, 'The ginger cat is my Dark Lady ...' In 'Reduction (Mr Milton)' and 'Reduction (Mr Wordsworth)', word clouds pulled from their texts become the basis for a further reduction—haiku.

These homages are not pious but playful, and Cresswell clearly delights in bending formal schemes and registers to light-hearted ends. The self-deprecating 'Undivined comedy' finishes: 'I took up pen and ink and page / and thought to write a wond'rous dirge, / but I am in my middle age / and ipso facto lost the urge.' 'In a Copenhagen graveyard' is more irreverent still, riffing on Shakespeare and revelling once more in rhyme: 'Goodnight, sweet Fred, / have fun being dead ... / may flights of fancy / soothe you in your bed.'

There are breaks in the jollity, however—and it is the poems without such a wink in their eye that I find myself most drawn to. (Perhaps I am a spoil-sport.) 'Battlefield' is lyrical, yet utterly frank about the harsh truth of impermanence: 'Fall's first love bite / nips leaves / not in the bud but / in their fullness.' 'Ingathering' poignantly crystallises the moment of receiving terrible news: 'No. We'll wait a minute, / watch the fireflies feint and fade.' Perhaps the darkest and most startling of the collection is 'Promised land', a prose poem in a voice that's chillingly clinical: 'Mix the poison with an appropriate carrier and spread it wherever wasps congregate. The best carriers are milk and honey.'

But however striking its darker moments may be, *Field Notes* seems concerned primarily with everyday beauty. 'We clean up bad memories / a penny at a time,' states the opening poem, 'Look to the ant'—and this collection certainly gleams.

Luminescent is Nina Powles' debut collection. The product of her master's in creative writing at Victoria University, in its first draft it garnered the 2015 Biggs Family Prize for Poetry—and it's not difficult to see why.

The physical collection consists of five brightly coloured chapbooks contained in a dark blue folder cover. As objects they are beautiful; there's something pleasingly tactile about opening a little folder of books. They may be read in any order, which is just as well, because I immediately took them all out and muddled them up in my enthusiasm.

Each chapbook centres around a different woman from New Zealand history, some better known than others. 'The Glowing Space Between the Stars' focuses on cosmologist Beatrice Tinsley; 'Whale Fall' centres on early settler Betty Guard; dancer Phyllis Porter's fate is explored in 'Her and the Flames'; '(Auto) biography of a Ghost' imagines the life of a school ghost; and 'Sunflowers' is a tribute to Katherine Mansfield. Historical notes are provided on the last page of each chapbook; and while I raced to the

back, impatient for context, it might be wiser to let the poems wash over you first. The historical specificities are undeniably crucial, but there's a universality at play here too. These are ultimately poems about female subjectivity, female experience; and they are as much about Powles as they are about Tinsley or Mansfield.

'Which ending would she have liked best?' asks Powles in 'Swan Lake', giving interiority to the dancer turned into a headline by her death. Powles' women inhabit different decades, centuries, social classes, fields of work; but they are all given complex, private interior lives. One such private moment of equipoise is captured in 'The echo': 'in the space / between / the inhale / and the exhale / she shuts her eyes / keeps it for herself'.

These women are not museum pieces for Powles; they are as alive and fully human as she is. They are, or have been, youthful; 'Penpal, 1957' gives us young Beatrice Tinsley in the form of a newspaper ad: 'Girl, 16, interested in wave technology, advanced mathematics, chamber music'. There's a constant sense of Powles reaching out to these women across the centuries: imagining them, identifying with them, interweaving and comparing their histories with her own:

> When I was fifteen
> there was swimming pool blue,
> mango flesh yellow
> [...]
> When she was fifteen
> there might have been
> pink blood foaming in rock pools

The poems range in length and style; some are erasure poems, fashioned from archive material. Throughout them all, though, there is a delicacy, a lightness of verbal touch; words precisely weighted without being spare.

This is a carefully curated trove of a collection, and no doubt there is more to come. In 'The Glowing Space Between the Stars' Powles laments, 'I have collected up so many astonishing objects / that I have nowhere to put them down'—but in *Luminescent* she has made a beautiful start.

A Little Less Simple and a Little More Knowing
by Philip Temple

Edmund Hillary: A biography by Michael Gill (Potton & Burton, 2017), 540pp, $59.99

A decade on from his death, we now have the first biography of Sir Edmund Hillary not managed by its subject. When journalist Pat Booth wrote a short unauthorised biography in 1993, Hillary refused interviews and told him, 'I write my own books!' Indeed, during his lifetime he wrote eight, including two autobiographies: *Nothing Venture, Nothing Win* (1975) and *View from the Summit* (1999). Hillary 'authorised' Alexa Johnston's lavish, heavily illustrated *Sir Edmund Hillary: An extraordinary life* (2005), derived from the Auckland Museum exhibition to mark the fiftieth ascent of Everest. Until his death in 2008 Hillary guarded his image well—and even beyond the grave, at least as far as Tom Scott's 2016 TV series, which reiterated Hillary's own version of his life. In reviewing Johnston's book (*New Zealand Books*, January 2006) I noted that it was essentially a hagiography and its subject's authorisation suggested a 'saint conscious not only of his gospel but also his congregation. It also begs the question, how would an "unauthorised biography" read? Is there any one yet alive who will live long enough to find out?'

The first challenge to hagiography came soon after Scott's television legend, when Lyn McKinnon's book *Only Two For Everest* (Otago University Press, 2016) was published. This provided the first detailed and objective account of the New Zealand Himalayan Expedition of 1951, Hillary's first foray into the Himalaya. Until this publication, accounts of his subsequent achievements on Everest and elsewhere had both obscured the contributions of the other three members of that expedition and inflated Hillary's role. McKinnon revealed his perplexing lifelong denigration of its organiser, Earle Riddiford, and one chapter of her book also recorded misgivings about Hillary's leadership and behaviour by participants in later expeditions. St Edmund did, it seems, have some faults. Does Michael Gill's new, and large, biography tread the pilgrim path or does it take a more difficult route up the sacred mountain?

Biographers generally bring to their texts a knowledge and perhaps closeness to their subjects, as well as their own special interests and occupational lives. Extensive research is essential, sympathy is important but devotion or antagonism unhelpful. Gill meets these criteria in interesting ways. A first-rate climber, he knew Hillary well, from the time he joined the Silver Hut and Makalu expedition of 1960–61 until Hillary's first wife Louise's death in 1975. In his Introduction, Gill writes that his friendship then 'continued in

attenuated form through to Ed's death ... He shaped my life, as he did so many others.' From his extensive research Gill also states, 'It has been a privilege to have entered his remarkable life' and that 'One of the fascinations of Ed's life is the way he handled his fame and came to be recognised as the person who best represented the "essence and spirit" of New Zealand.' This might be qualified as the male 'essence and spirit' of mid-twentieth-century New Zealand. Gill's sympathy here skirts close to devotion.

The book is influenced by the scope of his friendship, and he announces at the outset: 'The years after 1980 are too recent for me to attempt to cover them satisfactorily—the years of Ed's marriage to June Lady Hillary [sic] will have their own biographer.' There may or may not be a sub-text here. But it does mean that of the 500 pages of narrative, just 70 cover the 33 years following the devastation of Louise Hillary's death in a Kathmandu plane crash.

Gill's lifelong participation in and fascination with mountaineering, especially in the Himalaya, govern the structure of most of the book. His profession as a doctor with a degree in physiology, and his experience with the experiments during the Silver Hut expedition, also invest the text with detail about the effects of high altitude on human physiology and the development and use of oxygen on the world's highest peaks.

As biography, it is unbalanced by Gill's decision to devote 50 pages to all the early British expeditions to Everest. Here he is presumably addressing a lay audience who know little about Everest attempts, but I suspect a larger readership will be familiar already with the history and will have read such books as Wade Davis's superb account of the first Everest expeditions, *Into the Silence* (2011).

Gill's accounts of Hillary's own expeditions, although often drifting away from biography, do offer insights into his character. Looking at styles of leadership on the Trans-Antarctic Expedition (TAE), Gill writes, 'Ed could be authoritarian at times but he could also be very flexible. He would listen to other people and adopt their ideas if they were better than his own, though not always with an acknowledgement. [British TAE leader] Fuchs was more certain he was right.' There was a serious clash of personalities, and the blow-up between Hillary and Fuchs—when Hillary openly doubted Fuchs' ability to complete the Antarctic crossing in time—is well told and reveals Hillary's major misjudgement.

A biographer has to choose what to include and exclude, and a reviewer cannot always judge what source material has been available. But the account of Hillary's participation in the successful 1953 Everest climb seems incomplete without any insight into his relationship with his great friend George Lowe on that expedition; or what Hillary thought about the exclusion from the team of his climbing mentor, Mount Cook guide Harry Ayres, after he was first invited by Eric Shipton and then disinvited by the eventual expedition leader John Hunt. Although the participation in various Hillary enterprises of Canterbury mountaineering stalwart Norman Hardie is recorded, essential background information is missing: such as Hardie making the first ascent of the third-highest mountain in the world, Kangchenjunga, in 1955. Hillary's denigration of Earle Riddiford, who contributed a good deal to his early Himalayan success, is put aside with the sentence, 'Earle, with his "cool intellect", just wasn't Ed's sort of person.'

Some controversial Hillary actions are overlooked. For example, there was enduring bitterness among some TAE members over his decision to shoot all the huskies that had been crucial to the New Zealand survey programme in Antarctica, when it may have been possible to have them flown out or wintered over.

Publicly, and especially overseas, it had at first 'been natural for Ed to appear as an engagingly self-deprecating, even naive mountaineer from a small country'. After some years, 'fame might have gone to his head, but by now people loved him for his simple modesty—which by now had become a little less simple and a little more knowing'. Contrary to common perceptions, Hillary also enjoyed his knighthood and, later, 'loved being a Knight of the Garter'.

These insights indicate the real and singular strength of this biography. Gill's access to family archives and correspondence has allowed him to reveal the inner man, to give us a portrait of a rounded human being, larger than the Kiwi Hero forever commemorated on the five dollar note or of the man Hillary wanted us to see. In particular, the letters portray his close, loving and emotionally dependent relationship with his first wife, Louise. They explode the myth (again perpetuated by Tom Scott) that Hillary was so emotionally constipated he had to ask his future mother-in-law to propose for him. It was already a done thing when he returned to Auckland, via Melbourne where Louise was studying, after his extensive post-Everest peregrinations. Because he was about to go off on yet another Himalayan expedition, he simply asked Mrs Rose to liaise with Louise in fixing the wedding date while he was away.

Despite the train of expeditions, Hillary never enjoyed being away from Louise for too long and later involved her closely in the Himalayan Trust and its school and hospital projects for the Sherpa people of Nepal. One comes to understand their relationship so well that we can almost share the utter devastation Ed Hillary experienced on her accidental death, along with his younger daughter Belinda.

When I was in Kathmandu three years after the accident, I was told that the Pilatus Porter STOL had crashed because rods, inserted through its flaps to prevent them moving in high winds overnight, had not been removed before takeoff,

rendering it uncontrollable. Only two years ago, the Hillary family received a letter from a correspondent telling how, as a young man in South Africa, he had witnessed the Porter pilot's irresponsible behaviour as a bush pilot who never bothered with pre-flight checks. This pilot had gone on to fly for Royal Nepalese Airlines and the correspondent guessed instantly who had been at the controls when he heard of the crash. One feels thankful Hillary never knew of this before he died.

There is much to discover and enjoy in this book. Despite its imbalances and lacunae, Gill's biography contributes much to a better understanding of the Hillary character and myth and his place in New Zealand's mountaineering and wider social history. It is a keystone for the definitive biography to come.

Vital Nature Writing

by Tom Brooking

Totāra: A natural and cultural history by Philip Simpson (Auckland University Press, 2017), 288pp, $75

Since the death of Herbert Guthrie-Smith in 1940, there have been rumblings on the Arts side of the 'great divide' implying that New Zealand lacks good, specialist nature writers. Apart from Philip Temple, David Young, Alec Calder and more recently Rebecca Tansley on the Pacific, where are our Gilbert Whites, Henry David Thoreaus, or even Robert MacFarlanes and Michael Pollans? Such complainers are looking in the wrong places. Most of our top nature writers are, in fact, scientists. Environmental activists and botanists Alan Mark and Peter Johnston, along with Neville Peat, ecologist-turned-historian Geoff Park, entomologist-turned-historian Ross Galbreath, broadcaster and author Alison Ballance and Rebecca Priestley (on Antarctica), have all produced vital nature writing.

One of the best is botanist Philip Simpson, author of two masterful books on iconic New Zealand trees: *Dancing Leaves: The story of New Zealand's cabbage tree, tī kōuka* (Canterbury University Press, 2000) and *Pōhutukawa and Rātā: New Zealand's iron-hearted trees* (Te Papa Press, 2005). Both won the Montana Medal for best non-fiction book. His new book on

totāra is just as fine, being beautifully written and lavishly produced. Indeed, the illustrations, whether photographs, maps, graphs or charts, are worth the price of purchase alone. Sam Elworthy and his team at Auckland University Press deserve as much praise as the author for producing such a handsome book. The only real criticism I can make is that perhaps Simpson could have paid slightly more attention to representations of totāra in Pākehā literature and painting—though he covers Māori representation expertly.

Simpson begins the first of ten crisp, bite-sized chapters by discussing where the totāra fits in the natural world. He immediately makes it clear to a mere historian used to working with 'time's arrow' (shorter in New Zealand than most places, at under 1000 years of human occupation) that we are talking about 'time's circle', by pointing out that podocarps, a family of conifers, have grown on earth for nearly 300 million years. Somehow they survived the 'mother of all extinctions' that occurred about 250 million years ago when New Zealand was still attached to the supercontinent of Gondwanaland. The totāra's tough bark, its capacity to reproduce every two years, its biodiversity resulting from separate male (pollen-forming) and female (egg-containing) trees, its ability to replace damaged trunks (or 'epicormic' processes) and its complex internal chemistry have enabled it to survive New Zealand's 80–85-million-year journey through its many iterations—whether flat or mountainous, tropical or ice-covered. The country's numerous earthquakes and storms have also provided the relatively slow-growing tree with many opportunities to revitalise. Survival for so long against such odds, and the capacity to live for 1000 years or more, make the five species of totāra very special.

Chapter two focuses on how totāra grows. Despite the claims of the 1913 Forestry Commission that the tree grew too slowly to assist reforestation, it actually grows surprisingly fast in its first 100 years. Between that point and around 300 years it can grow to nearly four metres in diameter and over sixty metres in height. It then goes through another vulnerable phase before entering a venerable old age that, like kauri, can surpass a millennium, especially if it lives to 500 years.

Chapter three focuses on other plant and animal species that live on or adjacent to the tree. Because it grows across a wide range of environments— from alpine areas to coastal beach fronts—it attracts lilies, orchids, rātā vines, ferns, mosses, liverworts, lichens and fungi. Mites and spiders join other insects such as moths, aphids and beetles on totāra. Microsnails, lizards, geckos and bats are also enthusiastic tenants of the giant trees, as are many species of both native and introduced birds. The totāra is, therefore, a hub of biodiversity, providing another reason why it needs to be protected more effectively.

Simpson then moves on to the subject that most interested me: the very different attitudes of the two major waves of colonisers towards what is an extraordinarily useful tree. He makes the important point that Māori prize totāra above all the trees of Aotearoa/Te Wai Pounamu because its great height, its relative lightness (making it easy to hollow out), and its ability to resist the corrosive impacts of either salt or fresh water make it ideal for waka building. The pliable heartwood is perfect for carving, and many pou (posts with a head marking place), palisades, epa (posts) and maihi (bargeboards) in meeting houses, musical instruments such as pūkāea (trumpets), and waka huia (finely carved boxes containing huia taonga such as feathers and pounamu pendants) were made from totāra. So too were kumete (bowls) for storing water and cooking food. Later, pou haki (flag poles) were also made from totāra. The bark proved useful for making pōhā titi, or kelp bags, for preserving the likes of sooty shearwater, and pātua (food baskets).

It is not surprising then that totāra has a high profile within Māori mythology and cosmology. The first tree the forest god Tāne made was totāra, and stories tell of how permission had to be sought from him before forest giants could be felled. Many ancient logs were also declared tapu. Yet the awkward fact remains that the eastern Polynesians who became Māori burnt off something like half of the forest area they discovered, approximately 14 million hectares, mainly in the first century of occupation. Probably much of that loss was accidental as fires ran out of control; after that destructive start, the emerging Māori culture placed much greater emphasis upon revering and conserving totāra, which is now protected under the Treaty of Waitangi.

European settlers also found the totāra particularly versatile, especially for housing, furniture, fences, survey pegs, water wheels, bridges, telegraph poles and railway lines. Whole houses with shingle roofs could be built from totāra, with one large tree producing up to 50,000 shingles. As late as 1936, state houses included totāra in their construction. Churches too were built from it, and some early cemeteries featured totāra slabs as grave markers.

Pākehā destroyed even greater areas of forest than Māori, especially as lowland totāra indicated that soil was fertile. Much glorious timber was wasted as settlers burnt off vast swathes of forest to create pasture to graze sheep and cattle. One could say that totāra created the nineteenth-century nation: over a billion superficial feet of the timber were milled in 1904, the year of peak production. But the cost was considerable: settlers reduced the forest area from about half of the entire country to around 23 per cent. Further accidental burning, now caused by Pākehā, proved destructive of a tree that had little capacity to resist the ravages of fire. Such extensive destruction arguably constitutes a Treaty breach.

Once the big forests had gone, other factors reduced the totāra population further, especially defoliation by possums and grazing by cattle. Little wonder that Simpson concludes with an impassioned plea to increase conservation efforts. He concedes that governments since the 1870s have made intermittent attempts, but suggests little has been achieved outside of national parks, scenic reserves and sanctuaries. Simpson also acknowledges the increasing endeavours being made by various iwi to save the tree. Queen Elizabeth II covenants have had some success on private land, and individual owners have tried to preserve special stands of timber. However, significant gains were only made when the fifth Labour government banned any further logging of totāra in 1999.

Simpson suggests that much more needs to be done—as with the current crisis confronting kauri—perhaps by creating a national totāra park and by growing a new generation of totāra across the entire country. Totāra is also being considered again as a long-term plantation tree by dedicated individuals. But while protection remains piece-meal, practices such as removing trees to make room for centre-pivot irrigation booms will continue to destroy remaining stands. Farming must incorporate trees more in its future development, a change that is slowly gaining traction as part of the effort to clean up our waterways.

Simpson's wonderful book is a timely

prompt to save these magnificent podocarps. Perhaps a documentary on a year in the life of a totāra tree, modelled on BBC Four's 2016 documentary *Oak Tree: Nature's greatest survivor*, would help raise consciousness of the totāra forest's endangered state by highlighting just what extraordinary organisms giant trees are. Writers on the Arts side of C.P. Snow's 'great divide' need to take up their pens along with scientists: saving these trees is a matter of urgency. What better means of defence against climate change than planting more giant collectors of CO_2?

This book adds enormously to the understanding of our environmental, cultural and social history. A taonga in its own right, and a powerful educative tool, it should be read by as many New Zealanders as possible; and we should all call for a similar volume from Simpson on the kauri.

CASELBERG

Trust

CASELBERG TRUST INTERNATIONAL

poetry

PRIZE 2018

First prize: $500
+ one week stay at the Caselberg House, Broad Bay, Dunedin

Second prize: $250

5 highly commended
(no monetary prize)

The first and second placed poems will be published in the November 2018 edition of *Landfall*

Entries open: 1 June 2018
Entries close: 31 July 2018

For Conditions and Entry Form go to
www.caselbergtrust.org

future Landfall editor swots up

UNITY BOOKS

57 Willis Street, Wellington | 19 High St, Auckland
04 499 4245 | 09 307 0731
wellington@unitybooks.co.nz | auckland@unitybooks.co.nz
www.unitybooksonline.co.nz

RUSS FLATT

Remembering Forward
01 MAY - 02 JUNE 2018

TIMMELVILLE

4 WINCHESTER ST NEWTON
AUCKLAND NEW ZEALAND
TELEPHONE +64 9 378 1500
INFO@TIMMELVILLE.COM
WWW.TIMMELVILLE.COM

NEW BOOKS FROM
OTAGO

WALKING TO JUTLAND STREET

MICHAEL STEVEN

The exciting debut collection of an Auckland poet with strong connections to Dunedin who is an astute and sympathetic observer of gritty, day-to-day urban reality, and equally a writer steeped in literary tradition, Buddhist mysticism and world-historical narrative.

ISBN 978-1-98-853118-2, paperback, $27.50

THE WORLD'S DIN:
LISTENING TO RECORDS, RADIO AND FILMS IN NEW ZEALAND 1880–1940

PETER HOAR

New Zealanders started hearing things in new ways when new audio technologies arrived from overseas in the late 19th century. The World's Din is a beautifully written account of the arrival of these 'talking machines', and their growing place in public and private life.

ISBN 978-1-98-853119-9, paperback, $45

THE EXPATRIATE MYTH: NEW ZEALAND WRITERS AND THE COLONIAL WORLD

HELEN BONES

Many New Zealand writers in the late 19th and early 20th centuries travelled extensively or lived overseas for a time. The Expatriate Myth challenges the conventional understanding that they were forced to leave in search of literary inspiration and publishing opportunities. Based on detailed historical and empirical research.

ISBN 978-1-98-853117-5, paperback, $35

WHISPER OF A CROW'S WING

MAJELLA CULLINANE

This remarkable second collection is the work of a poet with a distinct and powerful voice. These poems weigh and examine oppositions – the distance of time and place, the balance of life and death, the poet's New Zealand home and her Irish heritage.

ISBN 978-1-98-853122-9, paperback, $27.50

Otago University Press
From good booksellers or www.otago.ac.nz/press

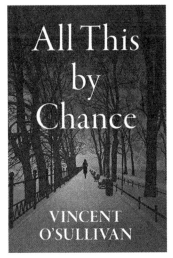

A moving multigenerational family saga about the burden of secrets never shared.
Novel, pb, $35

A mesmerising story of blood-ties that stretch across borders.
Novel, pb, $30

Stories about the deeply influential thread of Christian peacemaking in New Zealand.
Non-fiction, pb, $30

Elegaic and bittersweet, *Winter Eyes* is Harry Ricketts' best yet.
Poetry, pb, $25

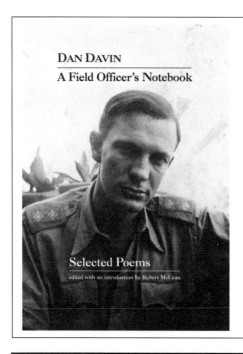

DAN DAVIN

A Field Officer's Notebook

Selected Poems

edited with an introduction by Robert McLean

'Quite unlike anything in New Zealand literature—exacting yet generous, angry but tender, almost *sui generis*—Davin's poems speak unguardedly and disarmingly about one man's life, his great loves and great many losses, in a voice that haunts long after it has been heard.'

—*from the introduction by Robert McLean*

'This is one of those rare posthumous publications that allows us to read an author we know from a new and more personal perspective.'

—*Vincent O'Sullivan*

104pp, $25.00

COLD HUB PRESS
coldhubpress.co.nz

The Otago Art Society and Otago University Press present

THE LANDFALL EXHIBITION

Works inspired by old
issues of *Landfall*

25 May–17 June 2018

Otago Art Society
Dunedin Railway Station (1st floor)
Phone 03 4779465
otagoartsociety@xtra.co.nz

Proudly supporting 'Landfall' and new New Zealand writing

University
Book Shop

Dunedin's Finest Book Shop

www.unibooks.co.nz [f]

378 Great King St + On Campus + Online

UNESCO
CITY OF LITERATURE
DUNEDIN

cre8ive7514

TE HUNGA TITO RURI O AOTEAROA

NEW ZEALAND POETRY SOCIETY

SUPPORTING AND PROMOTING POETS AND POETRY IN NEW ZEALAND

The New Zealand Poetry Society promotes, develops and supports poets and poetry in New Zealand.

We do this through:

- a fine line – our quarterly magazine
- The Annual International Poetry Competition and quarterly Instagram competitions
- The Annual New Zealand Poetry Society Anthology
- The Lauris Edmond Award for Distinguished Contribution to Poetry
- Supporting community poetry groups and poetry events

Join the New Zealand Poetry Society and help support poetry in New Zealand.

New! Student membership - only $15/year

www.poetrysociety.org.nz - Facebook NewZealandPoetrySociety - Twitter@NZPS - Instagram@NZPoetrySociety

CONTRIBUTORS

Aimee-Jane Anderson-O'Connor was recently announced as the co-winner of the 2017 Monash Prize for Emerging Writers. Her work has appeared in *Starling*, *Mayhem*, *Brief*, *Poetry New Zealand*, *Landfall*, *Turbine* and *Verge*.

Nick Ascroft has a collection of selected poems forthcoming in 2018 from Boatwhistle (UK), entitled *Dandy Bogan*.

Joseph Barbon was born in Palmerston North in 1995. He writes fiction and criticism and is a postgraduate student at Victoria University of Wellington.

Airini Beautrais is the author of four collections of poetry, most recently *Flow: Whanganui River poems* (VUP, 2017), which was longlisted for the 2018 Ockham New Zealand Book Awards. She is working on a collection of short fiction.

Tony Beyer's most recent book is *Anchor Stone* (Cold Hub Press, 2017). He is living in Taranaki and working on new poems.

Mark Broatch is a journalist, critic and the author of four books. He was a Sargeson fellow in 2011 and has been awarded a residency at the Michael King Writers' Centre in October 2018 to work on a novel.

Tom Brooking is a professor of history at the University of Otago and is working on an edited set of essays on culture and democracy, as well as a monograph on the making of rural New Zealand.

Danny Bultitude is working towards a master's degree in English literature at Victoria University of Wellington. Unlike his character he is actually quite claustrophobic, largely fetish-free, and has not been published before.

Brent Cantwell is from Timaru and lives with his family in the hinterland of Queensland. He has recently been published in *Sweet Mammalian*, *Turbine/Kapohau*, *Verge*, *Brief*, *Blackmail Press*, *Cordite*, *Landfall* and *Plumwood Mountain*.

Rachel Connor is a medievalist. She is a postgraduate student of English at the University of Otago.

Ruth Corkill is a Wellington poet and a recent graduate of the Iowa Writers' Workshop MFA programme. Her work has appeared in *Landfall*, *New Zealand Listener*, *Hue and Cry*, *Poetry New Zealand*, *New Welsh Review*, *Wasafiri* and *The Moth*. In 2018 she will begin an interdisciplinary PhD in physics, ethics and engineering at the University of Stuttgart.

Mark Edgecombe lives in Wellington and teaches English at Tawa College. His poetry has appeared once before in *Landfall*.

Lynley Edmeades' first collection of poetry, *As the Verb Tenses*, was published in 2016 (OUP). In 2018 she will be writer-in-residence at Massey University, and then Ursula Bethell Fellow at the University of Canterbury.

Chris Else is a novelist, a reviewer and a partner in TFS Literary Agency and Manuscript Assessment Service. He is the author of six novels and two collections of short stories. He lives in Dunedin.

Johanna Emeney's two books of poetry are *Apple & Tree* (Cape Catley, 2011) and *Family History* (Mākaro Press, 2017). In 2018 ibidem Press will publish her academic textbook, *The Rise of Autobiographical Medical Poetry and the Medical Humanities*, and she is currently working on a chapter on poetry for Routledge's *Companion to Literature and Disability*. Jo works as a tutor at Massey University and co-facilitates the Michael King young writers programme.

Bonnie Etherington's first novel, *The Earth Cries Out*, was published in 2017 by Penguin Random House. Her short fiction, poetry and non-fiction have appeared in various publications in New Zealand and overseas, including *Deep South*, *Guernica*, *Headland*, *Ika*, *Meniscus* and takahē.

Jess Fiebig is a Christchurch lass who lives for new words, cups of tea, sunshine and her wire-haired terrier. Her poems have recently appeared in takahē, *Catalyst*, *Poetry New Zealand* and New Zealand Poetry Society journals.

Russ Flatt (Ngāti Kahungunu) gained a postgraduate diploma in 2013 from Elam School of Fine Arts. His work is held in collections including Auckland Art Gallery Toi o Tāmaki, the James Wallace Arts Trust, Auckland Council and the University of Auckland.

Meagan France is an Auckland-based writer of European and Māori descent, born and raised in Perth. Her work has been published in Phantom Billstickers' *Café Reader* and takahē. Meagan holds a master's degree in creative writing from the University of Auckland, and is currently working on a collection of poetry and redrafting her first novel.

Kim Fulton is from West Auckland, has been a journalist and holds a master's degree in creative writing from Massey University. She writes poetry and fiction, and her work has appeared in *Poetry New Zealand*, the *New Zealand Poetry Society Anthology*, *Hue and Cry*, *JAAM* and takahē.

Ray Grover's *Cork of War*, which is about New Zealand in the 1830s and 40s, won the New Zealand Book Award for non-fiction in 1983. *March to the Sound of the Guns* (2008) tells at first hand the stories of four young New Zealanders caught up in World War I. Its sequel, *Province of Danger*, which carries the same characters through the 1920s and 30s and World War II, will be published in August 2018.

Bernadette Hall's latest book is *Maukatere: Floating mountain*, with artwork by Rachel O'Neill (Seraph Press, 2016). Her collaboration with Christchurch artist Robyn Webster produced the exhibition *Matakaea, Shag Point*. She lives in the beautiful Hurunui.

Michael Hall lives in Dunedin. Recent poems of his have appeared in The Spinoff.

Isabel Haarhaus is a writer and teacher who lives in Auckland. She holds a PhD in English from the University of Auckland and since the mid-1990s has published poetry, short stories, essays, art writing, literature reviews and articles.

Rebecca Hawkes is a painter and media studies researcher who completed an MA in non-fiction writing at the IIML in 2016. Her work has also been published in *Starling*, *Sport*, *Mayhem* and elsewhere: www.rebeccahawkesart.com

Aaron Horrell's short stories have appeared in *Headland*, *Alluvia*, *takahē*, *Turbine* and the *Whanganui Chronicle*. He is a staunch unionist from a small town and is almost certainly a narcissist.

Penny Howard is a NZ artist of Māori (Te Mahurehure), Irish and Scottish descent. She has a BVA and her work is held in various permanent collections including the Wallace Arts Trust, Foundation North, Auckland Events Centre and the University of Auckland. Penny has been a finalist in the Wallace Trust Art Award, the Adam Portraiture Award and the Walker and Hall Art Award. She is represented by Whitespace Contemporary Art Gallery in Auckland and also has work available at the Artist's Room in Dunedin.

Jac Jenkins generally lives a quiet rural life but recently has explored her limits—spending nine months in Australia's Northern Territory, then completing an MA in creative writing.

Stephanie Johnson is the author of a dozen novels. The most recent, published under her nom de plume Lily Woodhouse, is *Jarulan by the River* (HarperCollins Australia, 2017). She has also published collections of short stories and poetry, and written for the stage and screen.

Erik Kennedy is the author of the chapbook *Twenty-Six Factitions* (Cold Hub Press, 2017), and his first full-length book of poems is forthcoming from Victoria University Press in 2018. He is poetry editor for *Queen Mob's Teahouse* and lives in Christchurch.

Brent Kininmont's first book of poems, *Thuds Underneath*, was published in 2015 by Victoria University Press.

Wen-Juenn Lee studied English literature and media studies at the University of Auckland. Drawing from her experiences as a Malaysian-Chinese in New Zealand, she writes of love, loss and belonging.

Kathryn Madill is a painter and printmaker who lives in Dunedin.

Owen Marshall CNZM is an adjunct professor at the University of Canterbury. In 2013 he received the Prime Minister's Award for literary achievement in fiction. He writes fiction and poetry.

Zoë Meager has a master's degree in creative writing from the University of Auckland. She won the Commonwealth Short Story Prize (Pacific Region) 2013, and her stories have been anthologised at home and abroad.

Alice Miller's new collection is due out this year from Liverpool University Press and Auckland University Press.

Dave Moore completed the master of creative writing programme at AUT in 2016. He has a piece in the 2017 Cloud Ink anthology *Fresh Ink*.

Art Nahill has previously been published in *Landfall*, *Poetry New Zealand*, *takahē* and *JAAM*, and in several US publications including *Poetry* and *Harvard Review*. He is a physician and lives in Auckland with his wife and two teenagers.

Janet Newman was the winner of the 2017 IWW Kathleen Grattan Prize for a Sequence of Poems. She is a PhD student at Massey University. Her thesis looks at New Zealand ecopoetry.

Charles Olsen is a Nelson-born poet and artist. He moved to the UK in 1981 and to Spain in 2003. His most recent collection of poems is *Antípodas* (Huerga & Fierro, 2016).

Joanna Preston is a Tasmanaut poet and freelance creative writing tutor. She lives in semi-rural Canterbury with a flock of chooks, an overgrown garden and a Very Understanding Husband.

Jessie Puru is a Māori poet and mother from Auckland. She has recently graduated with a bachelor of creative arts, and is currently the intern editor for the New Zealand Poetry Society's magazine *a fine line*.

Jeremy Roberts is a resident of Napier where he is MC for Napier Live Poets. He has appeared at poetry events in many locations, and his work has been published in a wide range of journals. He has performed and recorded poems with musicians locally and in Texas, Saigon and Jakarta. His collected works, *Cards on the Table*, was published by IP Australia (2015).

Genevieve Scanlan is an MA graduate of the University of Otago who lives and writes in Dunedin. Her poetry has appeared in *London Grip*, *Poetry New Zealand* and *Rise Up Review*. She was a participant in the Fortune Theatre's 2017 Emerging Playwrights initiative.

Derek Schulz is a New Zealand poet, essayist and writer of fiction. His work has appeared in *Landfall*, *Sport*, *New Zealand Listener*, *Art NZ* and *Architecture NZ*, among other publications. His essay 'Why Would You Bulldoze This?' was recently published in *Forest & Bird* magazine.

Sarah Scott is a recent graduate of the MA in creative writing at the IIML. Her writing has appeared in *Turbine* and *Up Country*.

Charlotte Simmonds is a Wellington writer, translator and theatre practitioner. She is writing a PhD thesis on Soviet psychiatrist and neurologist G.E. Sukhareva.

Tracey Slaughter's poetry was shortlisted for the ABR Peter Porter Poetry Prize 2018 and the Manchester Poetry Prize 2014. She is currently working on a poetry collection titled 'conventional weapons'.

Elizabeth Smither's new poetry collection, *Night Horse*, was published by Auckland University Press (2017).

Rachael Taylor lives in Wellington and works in a school library. She loves writing short fiction and is currently attempting to write a novel.

Philip Temple is an award-winning author of fiction and non-fiction, often on the subjects of New Zealand history and the natural world. His early book *The World at Their Feet* (1969)

was a seminal work on the history of New Zealand mountaineering overseas. In the 1960s he undertook notable expeditions to the Carstensz Mountains (West Papua) and Heard Island (South Indian Ocean).

Lynette Thorstensen is a poet and artist living in the Auvergne, France. She began her working life as an activist with Peace Movement Aotearoa. She was also head of Greenpeace Australia and worked in senior roles across Europe.

James Tremlett was born and raised in Tāmaki Makaurau, of Pākehā descent. He currently lives a transient life contributing to environmental conservation projects throughout Aotearoa. This is his first poem for *Landfall*.

Chris Tse is a Wellington-based poet and occasional food blogger. His book *How to be Dead in a Year of Snakes* won the Jessie Mackay Award for Best First Book of Poetry at the 2016 Ockham New Zealand Book Awards. His second book, *He's So MASC*, was published by Auckland University Press (2018).

Tam Vosper lives in Lyttelton. He is working on a PhD with the University of Canterbury English Department, writing on the subject of Allen Curnow and the poetics of place. Among sundry other distractions, he also reads and writes poems.

Dunstan Ward's poems have appeared in *Landfall*, *takahē*, *PN Review* (UK), *temporel* (France), *New Zealand Listener*, and on the National Library's New Zealand Poet Laureate website. His collection *Beyond Puketapu* was published by Steele Roberts (2015).

Susan Wardell was born and raised in Dunedin where she teaches social anthropology at Otago University, while raising her two children.

Sugar Magnolia Wilson is a poet from the Far North of New Zealand, who currently lives in Wellington. In 2012 she graduated with an MA from the IIML. Her work has appeared in various online and print journals, and her poem sequence *Pen Pal* was published as an art object by Pip Adam and Emma Barns in 2013.

CONTRIBUTIONS
Landfall publishes original poems, essays, short stories, excerpts from works of fiction and non-fiction in progress, reviews, articles on the arts, and portfolios by artists. Written submissions must be typed. Email to landfall@otago.ac.nz with 'Landfall submission' in the subject line, or post to the address below.

Visit our website www.otago.ac.nz/press/landfall/index.html for further information.

SUBSCRIPTIONS
Landfall is published in May and November. The subscription rates for 2018 (two issues) are: New Zealand $55 (including GST); Australia $NZ65; rest of the world $NZ70. Sustaining subscriptions help to support New Zealand's longest running journal of arts and letters, and the writers and artists it showcases. These are in two categories: Friend: between $NZ75 and $NZ125 per year. Patron: $NZ250 and above.

Send subscriptions to Otago University Press, PO Box 56, Dunedin, New Zealand. For enquiries, email landfall@otago.ac.nz or call 64 3 479 8807.

Print ISBN: 978-1-98-853124-3
ePDF ISBN: 978-1-98-853125-0
ISSN 00–23–7930

Copyright © Otago University Press 2018

Published by Otago University Press, Level 1, 398 Cumberland Street, Dunedin, New Zealand.

Typeset by Otago University Press.
Printed in New Zealand by Printlink Ltd.

ARTS COUNCIL OF NEW ZEALAND *TOI AOTEAROA*

Penny Howard, *Haere Mai E Ipo*, 2017, graphite on paper, 1000 x 710 mm.